GOOD INTENTIONS

OGDEN NASH

Good
Intentions

BOSTON

LITTLE, BROWN AND COMPANY

CONTENTS

GOOD INTENTIONS

Adorable is an adjective and womankind is a noun,

And I often wonder why, although adorable womankind
   elects to talk standing up, it elects to put on its coat
   sitting down.

What is the outstanding characteristic of matinees, tea
   rooms and table d'hôtes?

Women, sitting firmly and uncomfortably on their coats;

Women at whose talents a contortionist would hesitate
   to scoff,

Because they also sat down on their coats to take them
   off.

What is savoir-faire?

It is the ability to pick up eighty-five cents in nickels and
   a lipstick with the right hand while the left hand is
   groping wildly over the back of a chair.

Yes, and if you desire savoir-faire that you could balance
   a cup on,

Consider the calmness of a woman trying to get her
   arm into the sleeve of a coat that she has sat down
   on too far up on.

Women are indeed the salt of the earth,

But I fail to see why they daily submit themselves volun-
   tarily to an operation that a man only undergoes
   when he is trying to put on his trousers in an upper
   berth.

THE CITY

Here men walk alone
For most of their lives,
What with hydrants for dogs,
And windows for wives.

What is life? Life is stepping down a step or sitting in a
    chair,
And it isn't there.
Life is not having been told that the man has just waxed
    the floor,
It is pulling doors marked PUSH and pushing doors marked
    PULL and not noticing notices which say PLEASE USE
    OTHER DOOR.
Life is an Easter Parade
In which you whisper, "No darling if it's a boy we'll name
    him after your father!" into the ear of an astonished
    stranger because the lady you thought was walking
    beside you has stopped to gaze into a window full of
    radishes and hot malted lemonade.
It is when you diagnose a sore throat as an unprepared
    geography lesson and send your child weeping to
    school only to be returned an hour later covered with
    spots that are indubitably genuine,
It is a concert with a trombone soloist filling in for Ye-
    hudi Menuhin.
Were it not for frustration and humiliation
I suppose the human race would get ideas above its sta-
    tion.
Somebody once described Shelley as a beautiful and inef-
    fective angel beating his luminous wings against the
    void in vain,
Which is certainly describing with might and main,

But probably means that we are all brothers under our
pelts,
And Shelley went around pulling doors marked Push and
pushing doors marked Pull just like everybody else.

A *Glossina morsitans* bit rich Aunt Betsy.
Tsk tsk, tsetse.

Everybody speaks of being patronized,

Yet nobody speaks of the truly irksome shambles which is,
 or are, being matronized,

By which I mean that there is nothing more impolitely and
 noticeably aloof

Than a woman of a certain sort sounding out a man of
 whose certain sort she hasn't yet got definite affidavits
 or proof.

She displays the great names of her acquaintance for his
 benefit like a nouveau riche displaying his riches,

And fixes him with the stare of a psychiatrist to see if there
 is one at which he twitches.

George Washington and George Sand and Lloyd George
 to her are Georgie,

And she would have addressed the Borgias behind their
 backs as Borgie.

She always wants to know, first, where do you come from,
 and second, do you of course know Babs and Bonzo
 Beaver there, which you never do, often for your own
 very good reasons, but you try to make your reply a
 polite one,

So you murmur, "Well I don't really know them, but I
 know OF them," and she at once assigns you to your
 proper side of the tracks, and it is not the right one.

When she discusses national affairs she doesn't talk exactly
 treasonably,

But she refers to that part of the nation which lies outside
 of New York in the bright tone of one referring to a

*little tailor she has just discovered who does altera-
tions very reasonably.*

*Please do not get the impression that a matronizing
woman causes me to froth at the mouth or slaver;*

*I only wish to notify you that whenever you want her you
can have her.*

Beneath this slab
John Brown is stowed.
He watched the ads,
And not the road.

Though you know it anyhow
Listen to me, darling, now,

Proving what I need not prove
How I know I love you, love.

Near and far, near and far,
I am happy where you are;

Likewise I have never larnt
How to be it where you aren't.

Far and wide, far and wide,
I can walk with you beside;

Furthermore, I tell you what,
I sit and sulk where you are not.

Visitors remark my frown
When you're upstairs and I am down,

Yes, and I'm afraid I pout
When I'm indoors and you are out;

But how contentedly I view
Any room containing you.

In fact I care not where you be,
Just as long as it's with me.

In all your absences I glimpse
Fire and flood and trolls and imps.

Is your train a minute slothful?
I goad the stationmaster wrothful.

When with friends to bridge you drive
I never know if you're alive,

And when you linger late in shops
I long to telephone the cops.

Yet how worth the waiting for,
To see you coming through the door.

Somehow, I can be complacent
Never but with you adjacent.

Near and far, near and far,
I am happy where you are;

Likewise, I have never larnt
How to be it where you aren't.

Then grudge me not my fond endeavor,
To hold you in my sight forever;

Let none, not even you, disparage
Such valid reason for a marriage.

THE SKINK

Let us do justice to the skink
Who isn't what so many think.
On consultation with a wizard
I find the skink a kind of lizard.
Since he is not a printer's whim,
Don't sniff and back away from him,
Or you may be adjudged too drunk
To tell a lizard from a skunk.

THE STRANGE CASE OF MR. ORMANTUDE'S BRIDE

Once there was a bridegroom named Mr. Ormantude
    whose intentions were hard to disparage,
Because he intended to make his a happy marriage,
And he succeeded for going on fifty years,
During which he was in marital bliss up to his ears.
His wife's days and nights were enjoyable
Because he catered to every foible;
He went around humming hymns
And anticipating her whims.
Many a fine bit of repartee died on his lips
Lest it throw her anecdotes into eclipse;
He was always silent when his cause was meritorious,
And he never engaged in argument unless sure he was so
    obviously wrong that she couldn't help emerging vic-
    torious,
And always when in her vicinity
He was careful to make allowances for her femininity;
Were she snappish, he was sweetish,
And of understanding her he made a fetish.
Everybody said his chances of celebrating his golden wed-
    ding looked good,
But on his golden wedding eve he was competently poi-
    soned by his wife who could no longer stand being per-
    petually understood.

THE ABSENTEES

I'd ride a cock horse to Banbury Cross
For giblet gravy and cranberry sauce,
Two treats which are held in reserve by the waiter
Till you've finished your turkey and mashed potater.

PAY TO THE COLLECTOR OF INTERNAL REVENUE

Dear Mr. Collector: In years gone by
Few have loved you as little as I,
Or lifted their voices and torn their raiment
And so begrudged the quarterly payment.
We waged our feud with ferocious joy,
You the Hatfield, I the McCoy.
Before December Seventh, you see,
You were You and I was Me,
But since the little men willed it thus,
Why, suddenly You and I are Us,
Just as Internal Revenue
Today is Internal Combustion, too.
Enclosed find check, my unseen friend,
And never was check more gladly penned.
It is somewhat less than an emperor's ransom,
But cash it quickly and spend it handsome;
Spend it on factory, fort or farm,
Wherever you feel it will do most harm,
For I'd like to export a present to Nippon;
Buy me a present, and make it a pippin.
We sent some gifts in twenty-three,
When their cities were crushed between earth and sea,
But merely nurses and doctors and food
To bind their wounds and foster their brood.
Their letter of thanks was suave and pleasant —
But this time, please, a more practical present,
A gift to be truly honored by
The truly honorable Samurai.

Consider how, nineteen years ago,
The children wept in Tokyo.
The little children hungered and bled.
The children were healed and clothed and **fed.**
The children had reason to understand
American heart, American hand.
Which of the children, I wonder, grew
To fly in the shadow of Kurusu?
An ingenious race are the Nipponese,
Their secret weapon, a flag of peace.
Mr. Collector, I ask again,
Buy me a gift for the little men,
Let me pay for part of a Boeing,
Keep a Martin or Douglas going,
Put the money wherever you choose,
In guns or rivets or hobnailed shoes —
Now I know what money is for,
It's going to let me into the war.
Here's my admission. Need to hike it?
Hit me again, my friend, I like it!

THE LOUSE

Robert Burns, that gifted souse,
Kindly immortalized the louse,
Who probably won't, when he is master,
Immortalize this poetaster.

I'LL STAY OUT OF YOUR DIET IF
YOU'LL STAY OUT OF MINE

I prefer charity to hospitality because charity begins at
home but hospitality ends there,

Meaning that eventually you have to feed your friends
there,

And you try to be both hospitable and methodical,

So you find out whose wife is currently on the current diet
from the current fashionable thirty-five–cent periodi-
cal,

And it is Mrs. Pulsifer, for whom a simple coddled egg will
do the job,

And you decide to feed the normal people squab,

And you wish Mrs. Pulsifer joy of her titbit to the ultimate
dreg,

And eight diners sit down to seven squabs and a coddled
egg,

And after two days of her three-day diet Mrs. Pulsifer complains of ravening pangs in her vestibule,

And hints wistfully that she craves solid food, be it never
so indigestibule,

And one eye looks Goya,

And the other paranoia —

Oh, riddle me this, I beg:

What guest do you think ends up with the seventh squab,
and what host feasts royally on coddled egg?

LIKE A RAT IN A TRAP

After various guesses at last I've guessed
Why in spring I feel depressed.
When the robins begin to play
Summer is just a step away.
Then hardly the summer has commenced
When autumn is what you're up against,
And once that autumn has muscled in on you
Winter is waiting to begin on you.
So spring isn't spring, but otherwise,
Just a prelude to winter, which I despise.

Roses are things which Christmas is not a bed of them,
Because it is the day when parents finally realize that their
children will always be a jump ahead of them.
You stay up all night trimming the tree into a veritable
fairyland and then in the joyous morn you spring it on
the children in a blaze of glory, and who says Ooh!?
You.
And you frantically point out the dictator's ransom in
building sets and bicycles and embarrassingly lifelike
dolls with which the room is checkered,
And the little ones pay about as much attention to them as
they would to the punctuation in the Congressional
Record,
Because they are fully occupied in withdrawing all the
books from the bookcase to build a house to house the
pup in,
Or pulling down the curtains to dress up in,
And you stand hangdoggedly around because you haven't
any place to go,
And after a while they look casually over at the dictator's
ransom and say, "Are those the presents? Oh."
And you console yourself by thinking Ah happy apathy, as
long as we haven't had an emotional climax maybe
we won't have an emotional anticlimax, maybe we'll
get through the day without hysterics, ah happy
apathy,
Ah may this Yuletide indeed turn out to be the Yuletide
without mishapathy.

Ah could this sensational lull but be permanent instead of pro tem;

Ah and doubly ah, if Christmas day could but end at eleven A.M.! —

But it doesn't, but the lull does, and here's something else you discover as you keep on living,

Which is that Christmas doesn't end for about two weeks after Christmas, but it starts all over again right after the following Thanksgiving.

I HAPPEN TO KNOW

Hark to the locusts in their shrill armadas.
Locusts aren't locusts. Locusts are cicadas.

To seals in circuses I travel on bee lines.
Seals aren't seals. Seals are sea lions.

I'm a buffalo hunter. Want to see my license?
Buffaloes aren't buffaloes. Buffaloes are bisons.

I'm too old to be pedantically hocus-pocused.
I'll stand on the buffalo, the seal and the locust.

One of the hardest explanations to be found
Is an explanation for just standing around.
Anyone just standing around looks pretty sinister,
Even a minister;
Consider then the plight of the criminal,
Who lacks even the protective coloration of a hyminal,
And as just standing around is any good criminal's practically daily stint,
I wish to proffer a hint.
Are you, sir, a masher who blushes as he loiters,
Do you stammer to passers-by that you are merely expecting a street-car, or a dispatch from Reuter's?
Or perhaps you are a safeblower engaged in casing a joint;
Can you look the patrolman in the eye or do you forget all the savoir-faire you ever loint?
Suppose you are a shoplifter awaiting an opportunity to lift a shop,
Or simply a novice with a length of lead pipe killing time in a dark alley pending the arrival of a wealthy fop,
Well, should any official ask you why you are just standing around,
Do you wish you could simply sink into the ground?
My dear sir, do not be embarrassed, do not reach for your gun or your knife,
Remember the password, which, uttered in a tone of quiet despair, is the explanation of anyone's standing around anywhere at any hour for any length of time:
"I'm waiting for my wife."

THE PANDA

I love the Baby Giant Panda;
I'd welcome one to my veranda.
I never worry, wondering maybe
Whether it isn't Giant Baby;
I leave such matters to the scientists:
The Giant Baby — and Baby Giantists.
I simply wish a julep and a
Giant Baby Giant Panda.

DO, DO, DO WHAT YOU DONE, DONE,
DONE BEFORE, BEFORE, BEFORE

There is a man whose name must be, I think, Mr. Ogle-
    thrip, and if you will bring me his head on a silver
    charger I will award you the hand of my daughter and
    a lien on my future salary,

And nobody has ever seen him but when you go to an
    amateur performance of any kind he is always sitting
    in the upper left-hand corner of the gallery,

And he has the hands of a blacksmith and a heart full of
    enthusiasm,

And compared to the rest of the audience, well Mr. Ogle-
    thrip is not as chusiasm,

Because seasoned amateur performance attenders generally
    weigh their applause carefully so as not to be either
    a spendthrift or a hoarder,

Because unless the performers of any performance are your
    grandmother or your favorite cousin or something
    your aim is to applaud just enough to not hurt their
    feelings and not enough to induce them to duplicate
    the order,

And some girl who once handed you a cup of cocoa at a
    church supper appears and renders an imitation of
    Fanny Brice imitating Gertrude Lawrence,

And your applause preserves the delicate balance between
    ecstasy and abhorrence,

And she is just about to resign the stage to the next per-
    former and everything is as right as a couple of trivets,

When hark! What is that thunder in the upper left-hand

corner of the gallery, can Mr. Oglethrip be driving rivets?

No, but he is clapping his horny hands and before you can say "Gadzooks,"

Why, the cocoa girl is back with an imitation of Gertrude Lawrence imitating Baby Snooks.

Mr. Oglethrip's cup has no brim,

Mr. Oglethrip is he to whom what is too much for anybody else is never enough for him,

If Mr. Oglethrip heard Will Hays sing "Trees,"

He would want a reprise.

Do you know a picture program that Mr. Oglethrip would find simply peachy?

A double bill in which each picture contained a dual role for Don Ameche.

I think it would be nice

If when you cut off Mr. Oglethrip's head to bring to me on a silver charger you would cut it off twice.

WHAT, NO OYSTERS?

There is no R in the month of May,
There's none in the month of June,
And the days of the dog, July and Aug.,
Glide past on R-less shoon.
Then where are you going, my pretty maid,
And what will you find to eat
While the oyster broods in inedible moods
In his lonely bridal suite?

"I'm going a-feasting, sir," she said,
"I am on my way to dine.
Let the succulent bivalve cling to its bed,
Methinks I am doing fine.
For the chowder laves the fragrant clam
In the old New England style,
And if corn on the cob with my teeth plays hob,
I'll remember not to smile.

The baby lobster scarlet gleams
Next a mound of fresh asparagus;
While the blue point dreams connubial dreams,
I'll munch till my veins are varacus.
Lo, luscious now as an infant's lisp,
The strawberry, tart and juicy,
And soft-shell crabs as sweet and crisp
As a nocturne by Debussy.

Though there is no R in the month of May,
And none in the month of June,

Nor the days of the dog, July and Aug.,
You can stuff till you're fit to swoon —
Who's that a-ringing the doorbell so,
Louder than doorbell ought to ring?
Why, it's half a dozen oysters, bowing low,
And their mouths are simply watering."

Up, up, lad, time's a-wastin', press the ignition.
If relief is not forthcoming, consult your physician.
Winnow your symptoms, but never discard the chaff,
And consult your physician, your physician deserves a
    laugh.
Explain that when you swallow so much as a coddled egg
    it sticks like a fishbone
Somewhere behind your wishbone;
Inquire why your eyes of a sudden refuse to be focused,
And what is the sound in your ears like a courting locust.
Your physician's a man of talents;
Ask him whatever became of your sense of balance.
Don't be irked by his suavity;
Tell how you walk with your legs braced wide lest you
    trip over gravity;
Tell him, too, that your gaze is fixed on your shoes as you
    walk, and better to tell him why:
That a too long upward glance would send you headlong
    into the sky.
Tell him straight that on such and such a day
They took the difference between down and up away.
Give him your problem to solve,
Ask him what to hold onto when under your feet you can
    feel the earth revolve;
Every molehill a mountain, every wormhole a crater,
And every step like the step at the top of the escalator,
And don't forget
To reveal your discovery that hair can sweat.
Go ahead, tell him;

Release the cat from the bag, let the doctor bell him.

Give the doctor the chart, show him the map and the
graph;

If relief is not forthcoming, it says right here on the label,
consult your physician, your physician deserves a
laugh.

THE SNIFFLE

In spite of her sniffle,
Isabel's chiffle.
Some girls with a sniffle
Would be weepy and tiffle;
They would look awful,
Like a rained-on waffle,
But Isabel's chiffle
In spite of her sniffle.
Her nose is more red
With a cold in her head,
But then, to be sure,
Her eyes are bluer.
Some girls with a snuffle,
Their tempers are uffle,
But when Isabel's snivelly
She's snivelly civilly,
And when she is snuffly
She's perfectly luffly.

THE VOICE OF EXPERIENCE

A husband at a lecture
Twitches his architecture.

He undergoes the lecturing
Like unanesthetized vivisecturing.

He's a glassy-eyed conjecturer
Of the ancestry of the lecturer.

Husbands hide in storerooms
To escape Town Halls and Forums.

They improvise In Memoriams
For speakers in auditoriums.

They regard as nauseous nostrums
Opinions delivered from rostrums.

They feel about orators' rhetorics
Like Cæsar about Vercingetorix.

They flinch as the fog of boredom
Creeps verbosely toredom.

Their collars grow more and more cumbersome,
And at last they essay to slumber some.

But this respite their spouses grudge them,
And if they nod, they nudge them.

There is none so irate and awkward
As a husband being Chautauquard.

I know a man whom because he isn't a doctor I think of
  as Dr. Fell,

And I do not love him for reasons which I am delighted to
  tell.

Although he is a good citizen and a respected vestryman

He is unfit to be either a motorist or a pedestriman.

His is the car always approaching just as you are about to
  step off the curb, but you don't mind him,

Because you plan to cross as soon as he passes, because the
  next car is half a mile behind him,

But with your plan he plays havoc,

Because you have forgotten that he moves at the pace of
  molasses in Reykjavik,

And by the time he is gone and you are ready to step on the
  street,

Why the traffic formerly half a mile behind him has de-
  scended on you with the speed and power of a husband quashing his wife's suggestions for the disposi-
  tion of the fleet.

Dr. Fell is he who when as a dutiful driver you halt for
  the red,

Stands on the corner with a newspaper buried in his head;

Until you start to start with the green;

When he steps in front of you with the carefree counte-
  nance of one who is beginning the beguine.

Such is Dr. Fell, and I fear that I shall never be a friend
  of him

Particularly as long as he parks his car in a two-car space
  with half a space sticking out at each end of him.

NO BONDS TODAY

Every time you buy a bond
Adolf has a stroke.
Why annoy Adolf?
Can't you take a joke?

Every time you buy a bond
Hirohito's harried.
Wouldn't you feel guilty
If he hara-karied?

Every time you buy a bond,
There's Benito's pout.
Is anybody cad enough
To tease a stylish stout?

Every time you buy a bond
The Axites see red.
Don't irritate the Axites,
Buy a drink instead.

WE DON'T NEED TO LEAVE YET, DO WE?
OR, YES WE DO

One kind of person when catching a train always wants to allow an hour to cover the ten-block trip to the terminus,

And the other kind looks at them as if they were verminous,

And the second kind says that five minutes is plenty and will even leave one minute over for buying the tickets,

And the first kind looks at them as if they had cerebral rickets.

One kind when theater-bound sups lightly at six and hastens off to the play,

And indeed I know one such person who is so such that it frequently arrives in time for the last act of the matinee,

And the other kind sits down at eight to a meal that is positively sumptuous,

Observing cynically that an eight-thirty curtain never rises till eight-forty, an observation which is less cynical than bumptuous.

And what the first kind, sitting uncomfortably in the waiting room while the train is made up in the yards, can never understand,

Is the injustice of the second kind's reaching their seat just as the train moves out, just as they had planned,

And what the second kind cannot understand as they stumble over the first kind's feet just as the footlights flash on at last

Is that the first kind doesn't feel the least bit foolish at
   having entered the theater before the cast.
Oh, the first kind always wants to start now and the second
   kind always wants to tarry,
Which wouldn't make any difference, except that each
   other is what they always marry.

THE SMELT

Oh, why does man pursue the smelt?
It has no valuable pelt,
It boasts of no escutcheon royal,
It yields no ivory or oil,
Its life is dull, its death is tame,
A fish as humble as its name.
Yet — take this salmon somewhere else.
And bring me half a dozen smelts.

THE HAT'S GOT MY TONGUE

A girl, oh a girl is a wonderful thing,
And so I am happy to say is spring,
And a girl in spring is the absolute works
But for one conspicuous item that irks:
That hat.

A girl in spring is a skylark's hymn,
An evensong in a cloister dim,
A moon in June and a dove in love,
But why the discordant detail above:
That hat?

The crocuses put their best feet foremost,
The softest, tenderest raindrops pour most,
Nature walks forth in a robe of dawn,
And you, my love, what do you put on?
That hat.

Purple the lilac and green the oaks,
Is spring the time for a milliner's hoax?
Your taste, methought, simply hibernated;
But what did I get when for spring I waited?
That hat.

A girl, oh a girl is a wonderful thing,
And so I am happy to say is spring,
And you are what I adore the sight of;
That hat is what I adore you in spite of —
Take it off and let's jump on it!

SLOW DOWN, MR. GANDERDONK,
YOU'RE LATE

Do you know Mr. Ganderdonk, he is no Einstein, he has
　　　no theories of Time and Space,
But he is the only man I know can be both the hare and the
　　　tortoise in the same race.
Mr. Ganderdonk's proclivity
Is divoty Relativity.
Put him behind you in a twosome or a foursome,
His speed is awesome.
His relationship to your rear
Is that of a catamount to a deer,
And while you are still reaching for your putter
He is standing on the edge of the green going mutter
　　　mutter,
But once through you in his foursome or twosome,
His torpor is gruesome.
He is a golfer that the thought of other golfers simply
　　　hasn't occurred to;
He has three swings for every shot, the one he hopes to use,
　　　the one he does use, and finally the one he would have
　　　preferred to.
His world from tee to cup
Consists of those behind him pressing him and those in
　　　front of him holding him up,
Wherefore the rest of the world is his foe
Because the rest of the world is either too fast or too slow.
For Mr. Ganderdonk there is only one correct pace and
　　　that is his,
Whatever it is.

CREEPS AND CRAWLS

The insect world appealed to Fabre.
I find the insect world macabre.
In every hill of ants I see
A governed glimpse of what shall be,
And sense in every web contriver
Man's predecessor and survivor.
Someday, perhaps, my citronella
Will rank with Chamberlain's umbrella.

THE SCREEN WITH THE FACE WITH THE VOICE

How long
Is a song?
O Lord,
How long?
A second?
A minute?
An hour?
A day?
A decade?
A cycle of Cathay?
Press the ears
With occlusive fingers;
The whining melody
Lingers, lingers;
The mouthing face
Will not be hid,
But leers at the eye
From the inner lid.
With the sure advance of ultimate doom
The moaning mandibles larger loom;
The seven-foot eyebrows fall and rise
In roguish rapture or sad surprise;
Eyeballs roll with fine emotion,
Like buoys rocked by a treacle ocean;
Tugged like the bell above the chapel,
Tosses the giant Adam's apple;
Oozes the voice from the magic screen,
A slow Niagara of Grenadine;

A frenzy of ripe orgiastic pain,
Niagara gurgling down a drain.
How long
Is a song?
O Lord,
How long?
As long as Loew,
And Keith,
And Albee;
It Was,
And Is,
And Always Shall Be.
This is the string Time may not sever,
This is the music that lasts forever,
This is the Womb,
This is the Tomb,
This is Alpha, Omega, and Oom!
The eyes, the eyes shall follow you!
The throat, the throat shall swallow you!
Hygienic teeth shall wolf you!
And viscous voice engulf you!
The lolloping tongue itself, answer your question!
The Adam's Apple dance at your ingestion!
And you shall never die, but live to nourish the bowels
Of deathless celluloid vowels.

A VISIT FROM DR. FELL

Dr. Fell is at the door, and I would rather have a visit from
    Herr von Ribbentrop or Count Ciano;

They might liquidate the family, but at least they wouldn't
    leave chocolate fingerprints in the books and coconut-
    marshallow icing on the piano.

Dr. Fell is notable for the southern-central section of his
    silhouette,

And he lands in your frailest chair like somebody from the
    ninth floor of a burning hotel landing in a net.

You know the room that used to be filled with bric-a-brac?

That's where he almost succeeded in carrying two children
    simultaneously pick-a-back.

Hitherto, the plumbing has functioned as sweetly as a hun-
    gry mosquito lapping up citronella,

But the plumbing is where Dr. Fell disposes of any un-
    wanted object, from an old cigar to an old umbrella.

Dr. Fell's little finger projecting from his glass as he drinks
    couldn't possibly be genteeler or archer,

But whatever glasses you had a dozen of on his arrival you
    only have eleven of on his departure.

Every man has his own conception of enough;

Dr. Fell will not only nonchalantly knock a half-com-
    pleted jigsaw puzzle onto the floor but nonchalantly
    carry off a key piece buried in his cuff.

Come on in Dr. Fell, you must take pot-luck with us, no,
    wait a minute, I forgot,

Today we can only offer you kettle-luck, last time you were
    here you ran the ice-pick through the pot.

Do you hanker for April showers,
Or a rarefied day in June?
Give me a grade-A May day,
And please deliver it soon.
I am weary of branches naked,
Creaking like lovelorn cats;
The earth underfoot half bakèd,
And the sun overhead ersatz.
Send me a balmy zephyr
To play me a rigadoon,
And I'll gulp of my grade-A May day
Till my hiccups hammer the moon.

I WANT A DRINK OF WATER, BUT NOT
FROM THE THERMOS

Have you ever spent two and a half of your three hours' al-
lotted shopping time hunting for a place to park?
Have you driven behind the lady who gives you the
right-turn signal and then cuts sharp left across your
bow? Has the truck driver terrorized you and the road
hog sworn at you?

There is solace in the bitter whimsy of the unknown genius
who defined a thousandth of a second as the interval
between the moment when the red light turns green
and the moment when the fellow behind starts blow-
ing his horn at you.

But have you ever lost your early start on a six-hundred–
mile trip and had to spend the night in an individual
wayside slum instead of the cozy inn at which you had
foresightedly engaged rooms because child A couldn't
find her absolutely favorite doll, and when she did
find it, child B hadn't finished plaiting her hair yet?

Then you will agree with me that an accurate definition of
a millionth of a second is the interval between the
moment when you press the starter as you begin a six-
hundred–mile trip and the moment when two little
tired voices inquire from the back seat, "Are we nearly
there yet?"

Then again, consider the other millionth of a second
which lasts a year, when Time stands still, and
Eternity in the lap of Infinity lingers,

Which is while you sit in helpless paralysis while child B
carefully slams the door on child A's fingers.

Take the battle royal whose results no bachelor need ever
    have computated,
Which is the struggle to sit nearest to the open window, a
    struggle the prize for which is the privilege of sticking
    the head and arms out in just the right position to be
    immediately omputated.
Yes, for the father of none to thank his stars I think it only
    behooving,
If merely because he has not to contend with little things
    who will descend from the car only on the traffic side,
    and preferably quite some time before the car but not
    the traffic has stopped moving.
Yes, he can roll along as confident as brass;
No restlessly whirling little leg will knock his spectacles off
    as he confronts a bus, no little hand groping the floor
    for a vanilla ice cream cone with chocolate thinga-
    majigs on it will suddenly alight heavily upon his gas.
As the father of two there is a respectful question which I
    wish to ask of fathers of five:
How do you happen to be still alive?

The firefly's flame
Is something for which science has no name.
I can think of nothing eerier
Than flying around with an unidentified glow on a person's posteerier.

TO MY VALENTINE

More than a catbird hates a cat,
Or a criminal hates a clue,
Or the Axis hates the United States,
That's how much I love you.

I love you more than a duck can swim,
And more than a grapefruit squirts,
I love you more than gin rummy is a bore,
And more than a toothache hurts.

As a shipwrecked sailor hates the sea,
Or a juggler hates a shove,
As a hostess detests unexpected guests,
That's how much you I love.

I love you more than a wasp can sting,
And more than the subway jerks,
I love you as much as a beggar needs a crutch,
And more than a hangnail irks.

I swear to you by the stars above,
And below, if such there be,
As the High Court loathes perjurious oaths,
That's how you're loved by me.

A husband is a man who two minutes after his head
    touches the pillow is snoring like an overloaded om-
    nibus,
Particularly on those occasions when between the hu-
    midity and the mosquitoes your own bed is no longer
    a bed, but an insomnibus,
And if you turn on the light for a little reading he is sensi-
    tive to the faintest gleam,
But if by any chance you are asleep and he wakeful, he is
    not slow to rouse you with the complaint that he
    can't close his eyes, what about slipping downstairs
    and freezing him a cooling dish of pistachio ice cream.
His touch with a bottle opener is sure,
But he cannot help you get a tight dress over your head
    without catching three hooks and a button in your
    coiffure.
Nor can he so much as wash his ears without leaving an
    inch of water on the bathroom linoleum,
But if you mention it you evoke not a promise to splash no
    more but a mood of deep melancholium.
Indeed, each time he transgresses your chance of correcting
    his faults grows lesser,
Because he produces either a maddeningly logical explana-
    tion or a look of martyrdom which leaves you instead
    of him feeling the remorse of the transgressor.
Such are husbandly foibles, but there are moments when a
    foible ceases to be a foible.
Next time you ask for a glass of water and when he brings

it you have a needle almost threaded and instead of setting it down he stands there holding it out to you, just kick him fairly hard in the stomach, you will find *it* thoroughly enjoible.

Why does the Pygmy
Indulge in polygmy?
His tribal dogma
Frowns on monogma.
Monogma's a stigma
For any Pygma.
If he sticks to monogmy
A Pygmy's a hogmy.

A BEGINNER'S GUIDE TO THE OCEAN

Let us now consider the ocean.

It is always in motion.

It is generally understood to be the source of much of our rain,

And ten thousand fleets are said to have swept over it in vain.

When the poet requested it to break break break on its cold gray rocks it obligingly broke broke broke.

Which as the poet was Alfred Lord Tennyson didn't surprise him at all but if it had been me I would probably have had a stroke.

Some people call it the Atlantic and some the Pacific or the Antarctic or the Indian or the Mediterranean Sea,

But I always say what difference does it make, some old geographer mumbling a few words of it, it will always be just the Ocean to me.

There is an immortal dignity about something like the Atlantic,

Which seems to drive unimmortal undignified human beings frustratedly frantic.

Just give them one foot on the beach and people who were perfectly normal formerly, or whilom,

Why, they are subject to whoops and capers that would get them blackballed from an asylum;

Yet be they never so rampant and hollerant,

The ocean is tolerant,

Except a couple of times a day it gives up in disgust and goes off by itself and hides,

And that, my dears, accounts for the tides.

LINES TO BE HUMMED FROM A SUPINE POSITION TO THE HUMMER'S OSTEOPATHIC PHYSICIAN

For him who botches
That delicate neck trick,
There waits, my friend,
The fauteuil electric.

DRIVE SLOW, MAN CHORTLING, OR,
APRIL, 1941

Gangway, everybody, hold your hats,
Curb your dogs and leash your cats,
Embrace your young in parental clasp,
Breathe in deep and prepare to gasp,
Feel your pulse grow rapid and joggly,
Open your eyes and goggle agogly,
Hitch your wonderment to a star —
Here comes me in a brand-new car.

Behold this gem of automobiles!
At either end it has two wheels.
What's more, you'll notice as you draw near it
Another wheel inside, to steer it.
Oh my, how I that car admires!
The outside wheels have rubber tires.
Oh bless the day that I was born!
The inside wheel supports the horn.

My natal day I will not curse.
I've three speeds forward and one reverse.
The backward speed I truly adore,
Yet love the forward three times more.
Upon this car I am a doter;
Golly, it's even got a motor!
Nothing so much a car improves
As when you start it up, it moves.

Pour forth, my soul, in joyous hymns;
The wiper wipes, the dimmer dims,

The body on loving springs is bolstered,
And wherever you sit, it's all upholstered.
The luggage compartment is so commodious
That sleeping in it would not be odious.
Doubt if you must, but I know I'm right, there;
As a matter of fact, I spent last night there.

Oh how I pity Father Divine,
Who hasn't a new car just like mine.
Kings and emperors make mistakes
Riding around in inferior makes.
Gangway, you motoring proletariat,
Here comes me in a brand-new chariot,
And I'll sell you my thoughts for one half of tuppence:
A lot of road hogs are going to get their come-uppance.

THE GANDER

Be careful not to cross the gander,
A bird composed of beak and dander.
His heart is filled with prideful hate
Of all the world except his mate,
And if the neighbors do not err
He's overfond of beating her.
Is she happy? What's the use
Of trying to psychoanalyze a goose?

A FRIEND IN NEED WILL BE AROUND
IN FIVE MINUTES

What are friends?

Why, they are people for love of whom one goes out and
eagerly borrows what one to them eagerly lends,

Who in return assure one that if one were about to be
eaten by an octopus they would dive fathoms deep
to the rescue at the risk of contracting the bends,

But who, if one faces any more prosaic emergency such as
asking if they would mind one's bringing along an
extra girl, one is making a mistake if one on them
depends.

They are people on whose entertainment one's entire in-
come one hospitably and hebdomadally spends,

And who at one's house eat birthright and at their house
one eats pottage and other odds and ends,

And for whose behavior one is to one's foes constantly
making amends,

Yes, that's what are friends.

What then are foes?

Why they are the least of anybody sensible's woes,

Because if there is one thing that you might of anybody
sensible suppose,

It is that he wouldn't have anything to do with people who
prove to be foes,

Because obviously if one tarries blithely among one's
proven foemen,

Why whom has one to blame but oneself if one receives a
poisoned barb in the small of the back or a poisoned
comment on the large of the abdomen?

Yes, friends are unavoidable and epidemic and therefore
    friend trouble is forgivable but I have no sympathy
    for him who circles Robin Hood's barn and exposes
Himself to foeses.
I maintain that foes are very nice people as long as a reason-
    able distance separates oneself and them, whereas a
    friend in need or in his cups can reach you across
    mountains of glass and lakes of fire, with which re-
    mark I shall now close,
Simply pausing to add that compared to a friend at the
    front door I find foes at a reasonable distance rather
    restful, and from now on I shall ever think of them
    as Comme Il Fauts.

A BRIEF EXPLANATION OF WOMEN

*Women have antiques
In their pantiques.*

There is one fault that I must find with the twentieth
    century,
And I'll put it in a couple of words: Too adventury.
What I'd like would be some nice dull monotony
If anyone's gotony.
People have gone on for years looking forward hopefully
    to the beginning of every fresh anno Domini,
Full of more hopes than there are grits in hominy,
Because it is their guess that the Old Year has been so bad
    that the New Year cannot help being an improve-
    ment, and may I say that they would never make a
    living as guessers,
Because what happens, why the New Year simply com-
    bines and elaborates on the worst features of its prede-
    cessors.
Well, I know what the matter is, it stands out as clear as
    a chord in a symphony of Sibelius's,
The matter is that our recent New Years haven't been New
    Years at all, they have just been the same Old Year,
    probably 1914 or something, under a lot of different
    aliases.
In my eagerness to encounter a New Year I stand ahead of
    most,
But only if it's a true New Year, not if it's merely the same
    Old Year with its beard shaved off and wearing a dia-
    per labeled New Year just to get on the cover of the
    Saturday Evening Post,
Because there are few spectacles less convincing or more
    untidy

Than 1914 or something in a didy.

I am in favor of honesty as well as gluttony,

And I don't want a second-hand or repossessed January
first any more than I want my spring lamb leathery
and muttony.

Well anyhow, come on New Year, I may not be able to
paint as capably as Rembrandt or Dali or El Greco,

But if you are a true New Year I can shout Happy True
New Year everybody! quicker than Little Sir Echo.

Some insects feed on rosebuds,
And others feed on carrion.
Between them they devour the earth.
Bugs are totalitarian.

They tell me that euphoria is the feeling of feeling wonder-
    ful, well, today I feel euphorian,
Today I have the agility of a Greek god and the appetite
    of a Victorian.
Yes, today I may even go forth without my galoshes,
Today I am a swashbuckler, would anybody like me to
    buckle any swashes?
This is my euphorian day,
I will ring welkins and before anybody answers I will run
    away.
I will tame me a caribou
And bedeck it with marabou.
I will pen me my memoirs.
Ah youth, youth! What euphorian days them was!
I wasn't much of a hand for the boudoirs,
I was generally to be found where the food was.
Does anybody want any flotsam?
I've gotsam.
Does anybody want any jetsam?
I can getsam.
I can play chopsticks on the Wurlitzer,
I can speak Portuguese like a Berlitzer.
I can don or doff my shoes without tying or untying the
    laces because I am wearing moccasins,
And I practically know the difference between serums and
    antitoccasins.
Kind people, don't think me purse-proud, don't set me
    down as vainglorious,
I'm just a little euphorious.

This is the witching hour of noon;
Bedlam breaks upon us soon.
When the stroke of twelve has tolled
What a pageant doth unfold.
Drawers slam on pads of notes,
Eager fingers clutch at coats;
Compact, lipstick, comb and hat,
Here a dab and there a pat;
The vital letter just begun
Can sulk in the machine till one.
Stenographers on clicking heels
Scurry forth in quest of meals;
Secretaries arm in arm
Fill the corridors with charm;
The stolid air with scent grows heavy
As bevy scuttles after bevy;
Like the pipers on the beach,
Calling shrilly each to each,
Sure as arrows, swift as skaters,
Converging at the elevators.
From the crowded lift they scatter
Bursting still with turbulent chatter;
The revolving door in rapture whirls
Its quarters full of pretty girls.
Soignée, comme il faut and chic
On ten to seventeen a week.
When One upon the dial looms
They hurry to their office tombs,
There to bide in dust till five,
When they come again alive.

Saint Patrick was a proper man, a man to be admired;
Of numbering his virtues I am never, never tired.
A handsome man, a holy man, a man of mighty deeds,
He walked the lanes of Erin, a-telling of his beads.
A-telling of his beads, he was, and spreading of the word.
I think that of Saint Patrick's Day, Saint Patrick hadn't
    heard.

The saint was born a subject of the ancient British throne,
But the Irish in their wisdom recognized him as their own.
A raiding party captured him, and carried him away,
And Patrick loved the Irish, and he lived to capture they,
A-walking of the valleys and a-spreading of the word.
I think that of Saint Patrick's Day, Saint Patrick hadn't
    heard.

He defied the mighty Druids, he spoke them bold and
    plain,
And he lit the Easter fire on the lofty hill of Shane.
He lit the Easter fire where the hill and heaven met,
And on every hill in Ireland the fire is burning yet.
He lit the Easter fire, a-spreading of the word.
I think that of Saint Patrick's Day, Saint Patrick hadn't
    heard.

Saint Patrick was a proper man before he was a saint,
He was shaky in his Latin, his orthography was quaint,
But he walked the length of Ireland, her mountains and
    her lakes,

A-building of his churches and a-driving out the snakes,
A-building of his churches and a-spreading of the word.
I think that of Saint Patrick's Day, Saint Patrick hadn't
  heard.

But the radio announcer is ever in the vogue;
He ushers in Saint Patrick with a rolling Broadway brogue,
He oils the vernal air waves with macushlas and colleens,
Begorras, worra-worras, and spurious spalpeens.
If Saint Francis had a sponsor, we would hear him as a
  thrush,
And Saint George would cackle cockney.
Saint Patrick, here's my blush.

DOWN THE MOUSEHOLE, AND WHAT
SCIENCE MISSED THERE

This is a baffling and forbidding world of disreputable international shakedowns,

And reputable scientists spending their lives trying to give mice nervous breakdowns.

Let us treat these scientists to a constructive suggestion on the house:

Have they thought to try their experiments on a married, or at least an engaged, mouse?

This suggestion is not frivolous or yeasty;

I want to tell them about a mouse I know, his name is Roger, who loses his mind at a twist of the wrist from his fiancée, later his wife, who first caught his eye because she seemed to him naught but, as he puts it, a wee sleekit cow'rin' tim'rous beastie.

Now, it is Roger's contention that to err is mouse-like, and being only mouse, though indeed his paternal grandmother was a mountain, he is all too often conscious of having erred not only as a mouse,

But as a mouse's spouse,

As a result of which when he is justly chastised,

He is, as a reasonable mouse, neither upset nor surprised.

It's a perfectly natural sequence, Roger says resignedly, that began with Adam and Eve in the garden:

Crime, punishment, apology, theater tickets, and eventual pardon.

What gets him down, he tells me, is when he has erred and doesn't know that he has erred,

When his conscience is clear as to thought, deed, misdeed,
   diet and word.
It is then, says Roger, that he is ready to pay the psychiatrist a lengthy visit,
Because he can't apologize without knowing what to apologize for, whereupon the coolness which chills him
   for whatever he has done that he doesn't know he has
   done grows all the cooler for the very reason that he
   has no idea what is it.
Worst of all, he adds in despair, is that while racking his
   brains to alight on what it can be that he erred about,
Why, he often loops an extra loop about his neck by apol-
   ogizing for an error that if he hadn't apologized for it
   she would never have heard about.
So there you are, reputable scientists, it is in trying to recol-
   lect and expiate sins that it never knew were sins,
That is why a mouse is when it spins.

JULY 4, 1941 — JULY 4, 1942

How many last year were careless boys,
And fire and thunder were their toys,
And over beach and farm and park
Their hissing rockets split the dark.
Their stars flew up like flaming birds
Of Liberty, too swift for words,
And cannon crackers wrote in smoke
The free proud thoughts they never spoke.
Today their firework's eloquent glow
Is understood in Tokyo.

VISITORS LAUGH AT LOCKSMITHS, OR, HOSPITAL DOORS HAVEN'T GOT LOCKS ANYHOW

Something I should like to know is, which would everybody rather not do:

Be well and visit an unwell friend in the hospital, or be unwell in the hospital and have a well friend visit you?

This is a discussion which I am sorry that I ever commenced it,

For not only does it call up old unhappy memories, but each choice has so much to be said against it.

Take the sight of a visitor trying to entertain a patient or a patient trying to entertain a visitor,

It would bring joy to the heart of the Grand Inquisitor.

The patient either is too ailing to talk or is panting to get back to the chapter where the elderly spinster is just about to reveal to the Inspector that she now thinks she can identify the second voice in that doom-drenched quarrel,

And the visitor either has never had anything to say to the patient anyway or is wondering how soon it would be all right to depart for Belmont or Santa Anita or Laurel,

And besides, even if both parties have ordinarily much to discuss and are far from conversational mediocrities,

Why, the austere hygienic surroundings and the lack of ashtrays would stunt a dialogue between Madame de Staël and Socrates,

And besides, even if anybody did get to chatting glitteringly and gaudily,

They would soon be interrupted by the arrival of a nurse
   or an orderly.
It is a fact that I must chronicle with distress
That the repartee reaches its climax when the visitor finally
   spots the handle on the foot of the bed and cranks
   the patient's knees up and down and says, "That certainly is ingenious," and the patient answers Yes.
How many times a day do I finger my pulse and display
   my tongue to the mirror while waiting for the decision
   to jell:
Whether to ignore my host of disquieting symptoms and
   have to spend my days visiting friends who have sur-
   rendered to theirs, or to surrender to my own and
   spend my days being visited by friends who are
   thereby being punished for being well.

I shall grieve, *I* grieve, *I* am grieving.
Abel is leaving.
Abel, the wise and the clever,
Is leaving, is leaving forever.
He goes to a wealthy tycoon
For an extra five dollars a moon,
Abel, the kind and gentle
Whose faults, if any, were minor and incidental.
North Carolina was his native heath
And the gold in his heart ran all the way up to his teeth.
Abel, the courtly and portly
Is departing shortly.
Never were white shoes whitened or tan shoes tanned
As beneath his caressing hand,
Nor the silver and glass so luminous
As beneath those fingers bituminous.
Did a faucet leak, did the furnace refuse to function?
Abel had straightened it out between breakfast and
luncheon.
Did a fuse blow, or a bulb flicker and die like the flame of
plum-pudding brandy?
He had always a new one handy.
Did a guest request a harpoon, a harp, a tarpaulin, a tarpon,
a turpentine hipbath, a hymnal, let the guest request
what he would,
Abel would either produce, or rig up something as good.
He could string a radio aerial
Or lay out a person for burial.
His voice dark honey dripping from an olden golden funnel

And his "Suh" was as good as a "Cunnel."
Farewell, Abel, good-by,
You recede from my misty eye,
You have left to join your tycoon
For five more dollars a moon.
O Abel, no longer visible,
Abel, I'm misible!

GEDDONDILLO

The sharrot scudders nights in the quastron now,
The dorlim slinks undeceded in the grost,
Appetency lights the corb of the guzzard now,
The ancient beveldric is otley lost.

Treduty flees like a darbit along the drace now,
Collody lollops belutedly over the slawn.
The bloodbound bitterlitch bays the ostrous moon now,
For yesterday's bayable majicity is flunkly gone.

Make way, make way, the preluge is scarly nonce now,
Make way, I say, the gronderous Demiburge comes,
His blidless veins shall ye joicily rejugulate now,
And gollify him from 'twixt his protecherous gums.

Please don't anybody ask me to decide anything, I do not
    know a nut from a meg,
Or which came first, the lady or the tiger, or which came
    next, the chicken or the egg.
It takes a man of vision
To make a decision,
And my every memory
Is far too dilemmary.
I am, alas, to be reckoned
With the shortstop who can't decide whether to throw
    to first or second,
Nor can I decide whether to put, except after c,
E before i, or i before e.
But where this twilight mind really goes into eclipse
Is in the matter of tips.
I stand stricken before the triple doom,
Whether, and How Much, and Whom.
Tell me, which is more unpleasant,
The look from him who is superior to a tip and gets it, or
    from him who isn't and doesn't?
I had rather be discovered playing with my toes in the
    Boston Aquarium
Than decide wrongly about an honorarium.
Oh, to dwell forever amid Utopian scenery
Where hotels and restaurants and service stations are oper-
    ated by untippable unoffendable machinery.

Once there was a man named Mr. Deronda James
And he gave over his life to names.
It began one day when he sipped first half a beer and later
    an entire beer,
And a drinking companion told him the difference be-
    tween Biedermeier and Meyerbeer,
And he considered it an omen
And he got interested in everybody's cognomen.
The day he discovered that the Barrymores' name was
    really Blythe,
Why you could have knocked him down with a scythe,
And he would positively purr
As he traced Joan Crawford back to Lucille le Sueur.
He made a new will cutting a canary hospital off with a
    dollar and leaving everything else to his kith
Because a second cousin told him about Mary Pickford
    and Gladys Smith,
And if anybody mentioned Robert Taylor he would super-
    ciliously murmur, "Who?
I suppose you are referring to Spangler Arlington Brugh."
Success was to Mr. James a dangerous drug;
I am afraid he grew a trifle smug.
Poor Mr. James, you remember how his clothes were found
    on the banks of the Rappahannock.
That was half an hour after a spiteful canary finally con-
    vinced him that Darryl Zanuck's name is Darryl
    Zanuck.

THE GRACKLE

The grackle's voice is less than mellow,
His heart is black, his eye is yellow,
He bullies more attractive birds
With hoodlum deeds and vulgar words,
And should a human interfere,
Attacks that human in the rear.
I cannot help but deem the grackle
An ornithological debacle.

NOW YOU SEE IT, NOW I DON'T

Some people look to the future and others look days of
    yore-wards,

But even they see more eye to eye than two people on a
    train one of whom is riding backwards and the other
    forwards.

I don't know how it does or when,

But anything interesting described by a forwards rider has
    vanished by the time it should have swum into the
    backwards rider's ken,

While, through a freak twist of the current

The backwards rider gets to see a lot of interesting things
    that should have been there a moment ago for
    the forwards rider to see but somehow they just
    wurrent.

Travelers have told me and I have believed them,

That such noticeable objects as the Mississippi River and
    the Sierra Nevada mountains have disappeared be-
    tween the time when the forwards rider pointed them
    out and the backwards rider should have perceived
    them.

There are those who in an effort to explain this phenome-
    non have developed a disturbing knack;

They sit forwards and look back,

While others to whom their vertebræ are dearer

Sit backwards and gaze on the fleeting landscape through
    a mirror.

But no matter what they describe

Their accounts never jibe.

When I eventually establish my Universal Travel Service
and Guide Ways
I shall advise all my clients who really want to see anything
just to sit at home and look sideways.

SO THAT'S WHO I REMIND ME OF

When I consider men of golden talents,
I'm delighted, in my introverted way,
To discover, as I'm drawing up the balance,
How much we have in common, I and they.

Like Burns, I have a weakness for the bottle,
Like Shakespeare, little Latin and less Greek;
I bite my fingernails like Aristotle;
Like Thackeray, I have a snobbish streak.

I'm afflicted with the vanity of Byron,
I've inherited the spitefulness of Pope;
Like Petrarch, I'm a sucker for a siren,
Like Milton, I've a tendency to mope.

My spelling is suggestive of a Chaucer;
Like Johnson, well, I do not wish to die
(I also drink my coffee from the saucer);
And if Goldsmith was a parrot, so am I.

Like Villon, I have debits by the carload,
Like Swinburne, I'm afraid I need a nurse;
By my dicing is Christopher out-Marlowed,
And I dream as much as Coleridge, only worse.

In comparison with men of golden talents,
I am all a man of talent ought to be;
I resemble every genius in his vice, however henious —
Yet I write so much like me.

There are some fiestas that the moment you arrive at them
    you realize this is not your night to howl,

Because your hostess is still patting sofa cushions in the
    parlor and your host is upstairs applying the styptic
    pencil to his jowl,

And you apologize for being premature,

And when your hostess snarls "Oh that's all right," she
    is lying in her teeth, you may be sure,

And you wish she would keep on patting cushions and let
    you go out and walk around the block,

But she just sits there asking how you like their city and
    looking at the clock,

And at last in comes another guest whose name sounds
    like Miss Ubblebub, which seems highly improbable,

And she is wearing a dress that she wore first as a brides-
    maid during the Harding administration and hair
    that hesitates between the waveable and the bob-
    bable,

And you may not have suspected your hostess of craft,

But suddenly she is superintending appetizers and you and
    Miss Ubblebub are off in a corner as snug as two bar-
    nacles on a raft,

And an hour later when the last guest has been cocktailed
    and canapéed you have certainly run, as far as Miss
    Ubblebub is concerned, your conversational gamut,

And when at dinner you find yourself seated next to Miss
    Ubblebub, I think you may be excused an ardent
    shucks, or even a quiet damut.

PLEASE PASS THE BISCUIT

I have a little dog,
Her name is Spangle.
And when she eats
I think she'll strangle.

She's darker than Hamlet,
Lighter than Porgy;
Her heart is gold,
Her odor, dorgy.

Her claws click-click
Across the floor,
Her nose is always
Against a door.

The squirrel flies
Her pursuing mouth;
Should he fly north,
She pursues him south.

Yet do not mock her
As she hunts;
Remember, she caught
A milkman once.

Like liquid gems
Her eyes burn clearly;
She's five years old,
And house-trained, nearly.

Her shame is deep
When she has erred;
She dreads the blow
Less than the word.

I marvel that such
Small ribs as these
Can cage such vast
Desire to please.

She's as much a part
Of the house as the mortgage;
Spangle, I wish you
A ripe old dortgage.

A supper party is something at which you arrive either long
before or long after the rest of the competitors,

And you broke your glasses on the way over and can't tell
people you know from people you don't know or your
creditors from your debtitors,

And you had thought your morning shave would see you
through and you suddenly realize that your chin is
growing shadowy, not to say tufty,

And you discover that you are either the only male in evening clothes or the only one in mufti,

And as if your spirits were not by now sufficiently dankish,

Well, you also discover that you alone didn't know it was
a birthday party and are the only arrival not to bring
in a package either useful or prankish,

But with the arrival of the cocktails your spirits are turned
from the swath and scattered for drying, or as the
crossword puzzlers put it, tedded,

Until you realize with a shudder that you received through
an error the cocktail specially mixed by the host for
his brother-in-law, who is notoriously light-headed,

And you choke it down, and not till the salad is served do
you recover from your croup,

At which point it seems that you have no fork left, the im-
plication being either that it now rests in your pocket
or that you used two forks on your soup.

But it is only later that the earth really begins to spin like a
fretful midge,

When it transpires that in this gathering of eight or twelve or sixteen *it is you and you alone by yourself who do not play bridge.*

You may well echo the words of the poet as you eventually wend your homeward way.

"Fate," said the poet firmly, "cannot harm me further, I have dined today."

August is sunburn and moonlight,
August's a menace to men;
When the casual canoer discovers l'amouer,
August has done it again.
August is moonlight and sunburn,
When the bachelor sows as he reaps;
His sunburn will finally unburn,
But he's burned in the moonlight for keeps.

Rainy vacations
Try people's patience.
To expect rain in the autumn
Experience has tautumn,
And rain in the spring and winter
Makes no stories for the printer,
But rain on summer colonies
Breeds misdemeanors and felonies.
Summer cottages are meant just to sleep in,
Not to huddle all day in a heap in,
And whether at sea level or in higher places
There are not enough fireplaces,
And the bookcase stares at you starkly
And seems to be full of nothing but Volume II of the life
of Rutherford B. Hayes, and The Rosary, by Florence
M. Barclay,
And everybody wishes they had brought woolens and
tweeds instead of linens and foulards,
And if you succeed in lining up four for bridge the only
deck turns out to have only fifty-one cards,
And tennis rackets grow frazzled and golf sticks rusty and
bathing suits moldy,
And parents grow scoldy,
And on all sides you hear nothing but raindrops going
sputter-sput, sputter-sput,
And bureau drawers won't open and bathroom doors won't
shut,
And all attempts at amusement fail,
Even reading the previous tenants' jettisoned mail,

Although naturally it would never have been jettisoned
If it hadn't been reticent.
But you could stand everything if it wasn't for one ma-
    lignant committee,
Which is the one that turns the sun on again just as you
    are leaving for the city.
Yes indeed, rainy vacations
Certainly try people's patience.

Your train leaves at eleven–forty-five and it is now but
    eleven–thirty-nine and a half,

And there is only one man ahead of you at the ticket win-
    dow so you have plenty of time, haven't you, well I
    hope you enjoy a hearty laugh,

Because he is Dr. Fell, and he is engaged in an intricate
    maneuver,

He wants to go to Sioux City with stopovers at Plymouth
    Rock, Stone Mountain, Yellowstone Park, Lake Lou-
    ise and Vancouver,

And he would like some information about an alternate
    route,

One that would include New Orleans and Detroit, with
    possibly a day or two in Minneapolis and Butte,

And when the agent has compiled the data with the aid of
    a slug of aromatic spirits and a moist bandanna,

He says that settles it, he'll spend his vacation canoeing up
    and down the Susquehanna,

And oh yes, which way is the bus terminal and what's
    playing at the Rivoli,

And how do the railroads expect to stay in business when
    their employees are incapable of answering a simple
    question accurately or civilly?

He then demands and receives change for twenty dollars
    and saunters off leaving everybody's jaw with a sag
    on it,

And when you finally get to buy your ticket not only has
    your train gone but you also discover that your porter
    has efficiently managed to get your bag on it.

LINES ON FACING FORTY

I have a bone to pick with Fate.
Come here and tell me, girlie,
Do you think my mind is maturing late,
Or simply rotted early?

O *She whom I cannot abide,*
Our hostess sat us side by side,
But must the heavy silence scream
Our heartfelt mutual disesteem?
Can we not mitigate our plight
If you turn left and I turn right?
This tasty fare will tastier taste
If by each other we are not faced;
Why shouldn't our acquaintance end,
Friend of a friend of a friend of a friend?
You do not love my way of life,
Myself, my children or my wife,
And too self-satisfied for tact,
Don't bother to conceal the fact,
While I my feelings may not hint
Till I can set them forth in print.
Our juxtaposition as we dine
Results from no intrigue of mine.
You'd wished yon titled refugee
Whose dollars Clippered here with he,
While I, whose hopes are mild and mere,
Had but desired to not be here.
Discovering who sits next to who,
Your face fell one inch, mine fell two.
Yet o'er our hostess's well-meant food
Did I refrain from being rude,
A minor courtesy which I grieve
To note that you could not achieve.
Well, Madam, if you wish it so,

Hitch up your girdle, here we go.
O living sneer, poor painted peril,
Yours is the snobbery of the sterile.
Three husbands have you unbeguiled,
And here you stand without a child.
Of hounds and huntin' you discourse
Who never sat upon a horse.
You, who have never penned a line
That would not shame a Bantu of nine,
Serve up the great as chummy nicknames
And little intimate make-you-sick names.
How glibly in your talk you glue
Bohemia to Park Avenue,
Unwitting that your gossipy speech
Stamps you a hanger-on in each.
Ah, let us our acquaintance end,
Friend of Hemingway's friend's friend's friend;
I'm just as glad as glad can be
To feel towards you as you towards me.

There would be far less masculine gaming and boozing
But for the feminine approach to feminine fashions, which
    is distinctly confusing.
Please correct me if, although I don't think I do, I err;
But it is a fact that a lady wants to be dressed exactly like
    everybody else but she gets pretty upset if she sees
    anybody else dressed exactly like her.
Nothing so infuriates her as a similar hat or dress,
Especially if bought for less,
Which brings up another point which I will attempt to
    discuss in my guttural masculine jargon;
Her ideal raiment is costlier than her or her dearest friend's
    purse can buy, and at the same time her own exclusive
    and amazing bargain.
Psychologists claim that men are the dreamers and women
    are the realists,
But to my mind women are the starriest-eyed of idealists,
Though I am willing to withdraw this charge and gladly
    eat it uncomplaineously
If anyone can explain to me how a person can wear a cos-
    tume that is different from other people's and the
    same as other people's, and more expensive than other
    people's and cheaper than other people's, simultane-
    ously.

MR. HENDERSON

There goes Leon
Glowing like neon.
He's got an appointment
In somebody's ointment.

THOUGHTS THOUGHT WHILE WAITING FOR A PRONOUNCEMENT FROM A DOCTOR, AN EDITOR, A BIG EXECUTIVE, THE DEPARTMENT OF INTERNAL REVENUE OR ANY OTHER MOMENTOUS PRONOUNCER

Is Time on my hands? Yes it is, it is on my hands and my
    face and my torso and my tendons of Achilles,
And frankly, it gives me the willies.
The quarter-hour grows to the half-hour as chime clings to
    the tail of the preceding chime,
And I am tarred and feathered with Time.
No matter how frantically I shake my hands the hours will
    not drop off or evaporate,
Nor will even the once insignificant minutes co-operate.
The clock has stopped at Now, there is no Past, no Future,
    and oddly enough also no Now,
Only the hot, moist, beaded seconds on the brow,
Only the days and nights in a gluey lump,
And the smothering weeks that stick like a swarm of bees
    to a stump.
Time stands still, or it moves forward or backward, or at
    least it exists, for Ex-Senator Rush Holt, for Doctor
    Dafoe, for Simon and Schuster, yes, and for Schia-
    parelli,
But for me it is limbo akimbo, an inverted void, a mouse
    with its tail pulled out of its mouth through its belly.
O, the world's most honored watch, I haven't been there,
    I've been here,

For how long, for one small seventeen-jeweled tick, or
    have I been sitting a year?
I'm a speck in infinite space,
Entombed behind my face.
Shall I suddenly start to gyrate, to rotate, to spiral, to ex-
    pand through nebular process to a new universe
    maybe, or maybe only a galaxy?
But such a Goldbergian scheme to extinguish one lonely
    identity seems, well, undersimplified and, if I may
    say so, smart-alexy.
Oh, I shall arise and go now, preferably in a purple-and-
    gold palanquin,
Borne on the copper shoulders of a Seminole, an Apache,
    a Crow and an Algonquin,
And whatever be my heart's desire, be it a new under-
    standing of Time or a cup of dew gathered from the
    spring's first jonquil,
Why if none of the other three will bring it to me, why
    perhaps the Algonquil.

I test my bath before I sit,
*And I'm always moved to **wonderment***
That what chills the finger not a bit
Is so frigid upon the fundament.

When speaking of people and their beliefs I wear my belief on my sleeve;

I believe that people believe what they believe they believe.

When people reject a truth or an untruth it is not because it is a truth or an untruth that they reject it,

No, if it isn't in accord with their beliefs in the first place they simply say, "Nothing doing," and refuse to inspect it.

Likewise when they embrace a truth or an untruth it is not for either its truth or its mendacity,

But simply because they have believed it all along and therefore regard the embrace as a tribute to their own fair-mindedness and sagacity.

These are enlightened days in which you can get hot water and cold water out of the same spigot,

And everybody has something about which they are proud to be broad-minded but they also have other things about which you would be wasting your breath if you tried to convince them that they were a bigot,

And I have no desire to get ugly,

But I cannot help mentioning that the door of a bigoted mind opens outwards so that the only result of the pressure of facts upon it is to close it more snugly.

Naturally I am not pointing a finger at me,

But I must admit that I find Mr. Ickes or any other speaker far more convincing when I agree with him than when I disagree.

NO, NO, NOVEMBER

Thirty days November hath,
Unfit for human living,
Including one Election Day,
And a hide-and-seek Thanksgiving.
An encouraging month November is
For burglary and mayhem;
It's night for most of the afternoon,
And P.M. *most of the* A.M.
There may be virtues in November,
But if there are I can't remember.

THE STRANGE CASE OF MR. NIOBOB'S
TRANSMOGRIFICATION

Listen motorists, and learn:

Once there was a motorist named Mr. Niobob who took
a trip from which he didn't return.

His first five miles were simply seraphic

Because he was on a dual highway and there wasn't even
a smattering of traffic

But then he had to leave the dual highway because his
destination was merely New York,

And dual highways never go to anybody's destination,
they all lead to a deserted traffic circle in Yoakum
Corners or Medicine Fork,

So Mr. Niobob turned off the trafficless dual highway
and with his usual luck,

Well yes, he immediately found himself behind a truck,

And whenever to pass it he mustered his nerve

Well, naturally, they came to a curve,

And it also bored him

That whenever the road straightened out and he edged
over for a dash there would be another truck clatter-
ing toward him,

And he wished he had picked up a little voodoo on his
cruise to Haiti,

Because while the truck bogged down to three miles per
hour on the way uphill, why when he thought to over-
take it on the way down it accelerated to eighty,

And all of a sudden they again entered a dual highway,

And Mr. Niobob said, "By gum, now I can drive my way,"

And he stepped on the gas with all his might,

And just as he overtook the truck it turned down a side
    road on the right.
Poor frustrated Mr. Niobob, his mind slipped quietly over
    the brink,
He just sat down and cried and cried until a kind Com-
    missioner of Motor Vehicles took pity on him and
    transformed him into a fountain, at which tired truck
    drivers often pause to drink.

This is the Lackadaisical Broadcasting Company, the
    Friendly Voice that also stands and waits,

Bringing you our annual Thanksgiving message through
    the courtesy of the President and merchants of the
    United States.

Let us now give thanks for the happy circumstances that
    led to the friendship of Mr. Sears with Mr. Roebuck
    and Mr. Montgomery with Mr. Ward, to say nothing
    of the concatenation of Messrs. Barton, Durstine and
    Osborn and Mr. Batten,

And for not being in a bewildered state on the Jamaica
    platform of the Long Island Railroad and about to
    step into the train bound for Atlantic Avenue, Brook-
    lyn, instead of the Pennsylvania Station, Manhattan.

Let us give thanks that women's wedge shoes weren't in-
    vented until they were,

And that the bad manners of the younger generation
    help middle-aged people to grow old without self-
    consciousness because they no longer shock you into
    a realization of your advanced age by offering you
    their chair and calling you Sir.

Yes, and let us consider that even if a lot of barytones sing
    "The Road to Mandalay" and "Danny Deever" at
    least very few of them sing "Gunga Din,"

And that a batter hitting a long fly with a man on third
    no longer gets credit for a sacrifice but only for a run
    batted in.

Let us also remember with affection the confused Demo-
    cratic delegate who spoke into the Chicago micro-

phone saying, "I want to thank the Chair for its recognichigan of the State of Michigan."

He was indeed an engaging politichigan.

So the Lackadaisical Broadcasting Co. bids you farewell with the message that if you aren't grateful to be living in a world where so many things to be grateful for are yours as a matter of course

Why it is now five seconds until fifteen minutes before eleven o'clock and you are just an old Trojan horse.

FOR DR. WARREN ADAMS, WHO KINDLY
BOUND THE AUTHOR FAR BEYOND
HIS DESERTS

I'm prideful to the point of sin
About my new and handsome skin.
How can a Muse resist when wooed
By one so tastefully tattooed?

Some people shave before bathing,

And about people who bathe before shaving they are
scathing,

While those who bathe before shaving,

Well, they imply that those who shave before bathing are
misbehaving.

Suppose you shave before bathing, well the advantage is
that you don't have to make a special job of washing
the lather off afterwards, it just floats off with the rest
of your accumulations in the tub,

But the disadvantage is that before bathing your skin is
hard and dry and your beard confronts the razor like
a grizzly bear defending its cub.

Well then, suppose you bathe before shaving, well the
advantage is that after bathing your skin is soft and
moist, and your beard positively begs for the blade,

But the disadvantage is that to get the lather off you have
to wash your face all over again at the basin almost
immediately after washing it in the tub, which is a
duplication of effort that leaves me spotless but dis-
mayed.

The referee reports, gentlemen, that Fate has loaded the
dice,

Since your only choice is between walking around all day
with a sore chin or washing your face twice,

So I will now go and get a shave from a smug man in a crisp
white coat,

And I will disrupt his smugness by asking him about his private life, does he bathe before shaving or shave before bathing, and then I will die either of laughing or of a clean cut throat.

"Who is that most attractive man?"
The eager people shout —
More shame on they,
For I'm sorry to say
It's Obadiah Stout.
The dowager swaps him compliments,
While the debutante admires;
They rock the globe
With praise of Obe,
The man with four new tires.

Last year he rode downtown alone,
And home alone from dances,
And girls in hordes
With loud O Lords!
Rebuffed his wistful glances.
He humbly crept from snub to snub,
The lowliest of pariahs;
No gaffer or youth
Foresaw, forsooth,
Those tires of Obadiah's.

The two in front are firm to touch,
Their pressure is twenty-eight–pound;
At the turn of a wheel
They never, never squeal;
And the two in back are round.
Oh, others must hobble upon the rim,
Or trudge, as did their sires,

Or swallow their pride
And thumb a ride
From the man with four new tires.

The upper crust of the crème de la crème
Hangs on him like a tassel;
The erstwhile bore,
The yokel of yore,
Is now the king of the castle.
For if you do not care to drive
In a jeep, or a Black Maria,
Or take a chance
In an ambulance,
You cultivate Obadiah.

How many hitherto gelid hearts
Glow now with amorous fires!
What traps are planned
For the fair white hand
Of the man with four new tires!
But hark! I hear from the beauty shops
A scream like a wounded cougar —
He has married a girl
With a winsome curl,
And a hundred pounds of sougar.

JUST WRAP IT UP, AND I'LL THROW IT AWAY LATER

Men think that men have more sense than women and
    women think that any woman has more sense than
    any man,

An issue which I eagerly evade, for who am I to pass judg-
    ment on the comparative reasoning processes of, say,
    Mr. Lunt and Miss Fontanne?

However, I ask you to visualize, please, a clear-thinking
    American male who needs a hat, or a left sock, or an
    ashtray in the form of the statue Civic Virtue by the
    sculptor MacMonnies,

And what does he do, he goes into the likeliest shop and
    buys it and returns to the regular evening race with
    the children for first go at the funnies.

Kindly contrast this with the procedure of his wife or sister
    or aunt who drops into a store for three ounces of flax
    for the spinning wheel or an extra minuet for the
    spinet,

And what happens, the doorstep is crawling for days with
    people delivering lampshades and bedspreads and
    dirndls and chairs that expand into bridge tables and
    bridge tables that expand into chaises longues, and
    husbands who can't bear it simply have to grin it.

Man's idea of shopping is to buy what he needs and get
    through with it.

Woman's idea is to have everything she has never needed
    sent home and then figure out what to do with it.

It is as true today as in the day of David and Goliath or
    Corbett and Fitzsimmons,

That men go into a shop to supply a want, and women principally to stimulate their imaginations, but men's imaginations need no extra stimulus as long as their world is filled with beautiful unanswerable womens.

ANATOMICAL REFLECTION

Sally Rand
Needs an extra hand.

Some people relate anecdotes about Samuel Goldwyn and
    Gregory Ratoff;

I sing of Dr. Fell, who slips in the only vacant barber chair
    while you are taking your hat off.

Does a young man go to a picture with a girl he hopes to
    make a bride of?

The immovable Dr. Fell is what the only two empty seats
    are one on each side of.

You are marooned downtown on a night when the rain is a
    Niagara and the wind is a bayonet,

And after twenty minutes of futile whistling you catch a
    taxi driver's eye and as he slows down Dr. Fell
    emerges miraculously from a hydrant, steps into the
    cab and drives away in it.

Dr. Fell obviously works with the assistance of a brownie or
    a malevolent dwarf,

For it is he who by monopolizing the middle of the road
    reaches the ferry ahead of you and slides into the last
    space, thus leaving you to two hours' uninterrupted
    contemplation of the wharf.

Yes, I fear that Dr. Fell is a monopolist and an obstruc-
    tionist,

But I would not grudge him the obstructive monopoly of
    that portion of a whirlpool where the suction is the
    suctionest.

THE STRANGE CASE OF MR. PAUNCEFOOT'S BROAD MIND

Once there was a man named Mr. Pauncefoot to whom
    Fate could not have been meaner,
Because he was a born in-betweener.
Yes, he was one whom in an argument nothing but woe
    ever betides,
Because he always thought that there was much to be said
    on both sides,
With the result that to his friends on the Left he was but a
    little capitalistic bee busy distributing Tory pollen,
While on the Right he was rumored to be in the pay of
    Stalin.
Mr. Pauncefoot lived in a suburb, which was inevitable
    but rather a pity,
Since the upshot was that he appeared as a city boy in the
    country and a country boy in the city.
He was never invited to sing either solo or in a convivial
    quartet by even the kindest Samaritan,
Because his voice was just a little too low for the tenor and
    just a little too high for the baritan.
Mr. Pauncefoot was miserable until one day he read about
    the donkey that starved to death between two hay-
    stacks because it couldn't decide which haystack to
    begin on, and he said, "That's an end of all my con-
    fusions,"
Only Mr. Pauncefoot didn't starve to death, quite the op-
    posite, he spent the rest of his days very happily eat-
    ing his own words between two conclusions.

WHAT STREET IS THIS, DRIVER?

Let this be my tardy farewell
To the erstwhile Sixth Avenue El.
Though no longer a native New Yorker
My æsthetic eye is a corker;
The El had a twelve-foot clearance
And I notice its disappearance.
New York was to many a kingdom
Where business or pleasure bringdom,
But I got there so seldom
To me 'twas Sixth Avenue Eldom.
It never got anyone downer
Than this timid out-of-towner;
It ran like an iron entrail
Midway 'twixt Penn and Grand Central;
It staggered column by column
From the Battery up to Harlem,
And no matter wherever went you
The Sixth Avenue El went too.
You'd be riding from Park to Madison
While leafing through Steele or Addison,
And fleeter than meter could tell
You'd be twisting under the El;
Be you headed south or north
On Lexington, Park or Fourth
Any whither you wished to flit,
Lay the El between you and it.
Farewell, O El, farewell;
I was once of your clientele.
Although I'm no longer Manhattanized

I'm glad that we met and fraternized.
I remember warmly enough
The journeys to Coogan's Bluff,
And the tingling tangling nerve
As we rattled round Suicide Curve;
You could tell by the chuckling sound
That the train was Giant bound.
There was Laughing Larry Doyle
In the days when oil was oil,
And later, when oil was fusel,
We hollered for Emil Meusel.
McGeehan wrote better than Shelley
In descriptions of Long George Kelly;
Hoyt was adroit and hot
And Ott a promising tot,
And I'd rather have met Frankie Frisch
Than marry Lillian Gish;
To win was the only law
And the law was John McGraw.
Ah, then we placed our reliance
On the El and on the Giants;
Now the El with McGraw is buried,
And the torrid Giants are terried,
Now realtors along Sixth Avenue
Anticipate mounting revenue.
No more the El careens
Past intimate family scenes;
Housewives no longer gape
From window and fire escape
At passengers packed like pemmican

Who are gaping back at them again;
Like Wichita, or Los Angeles,
Sixth Ave. is now new-fangelous,
Light as an air by Bizet,
And broad as the Champs Elysées.
Fit for Geddes (Norman Bel)
Is Sixth Avenue minus the El.
This notable civic improvement
Facilitates traffic movement;
It clears the street for sleighs
And the sidewalks for cafés.
O El, thy era is o'er;
I am glad that thou art no more;
But I'd hold myself lower than dirt
Weren't I glad that once thou wert.

SUMMER SERENADE

When the thunder stalks the sky,
When tickle-footed walks the fly,
When shirt is wet and throat is dry,
Look, my darling, that's July.

Though the grassy lawn be leather,
And prickly temper tug the tether,
Shall we postpone our love for weather?
If we must melt, let's melt together!

SO DOES EVERYBODY ELSE, ONLY NOT
SO MUCH

O all ye exorcizers come and exorcize now, and ye clergy-
men draw nigh and clerge,

For I wish to be purged of an urge.

It is an irksome urge, compounded of nettles and glue,

And it is turning all my friends back into acquaintances,
and all my acquaintances into people who look the
other way when I heave into view.

It is an indication that my mental buttery is butterless and
my mental larder lardless,

And it consists not of "Stop me if you've heard this one,"
but of "I know you've heard this one because I told it
to you myself, but I'm going to tell it to you again
regardless,"

Yes I fear I am living beyond my mental means

When I realize that it is not only anecdotes that I reiterate
but what is far worse, summaries of radio programs
and descriptions of cartoons in newspapers and maga-
zines.

I want to resist but I cannot resist recounting the bright
sayings of celebrities that everybody already is familiar with every word of;

I want to refrain but cannot refrain from telling the same
audience on two successive evenings the same little
snatches of domestic gossip about people I used to
know that they have never heard of.

When I remember some titillating episode of my childhood I figure that if it's worth narrating once it's worth

narrating twice, in spite of lackluster eyes and droop-
ing jaws,

And indeed I have now worked my way backward from
titillating episodes in my own childhood to titillating
episodes in the childhood of my parents or even my
parents-in-laws,

And what really turns my corpuscles to ice,

I carry around clippings and read them to people twice.

And I know what I am doing while I am doing it and I
don't want to do it but I can't help doing it and I
am just another Ancient Mariner,

And the prospects for my future social life couldn't possibly be barrener.

Did I tell you that the prospects for my future social life
couldn't possibly be barrener?

Be careful not to hate the moth,
It isn't she who eats your cloth,
But only little ones of hers
That lunch on tweeds and dine on furs.
Who but a jingo his heart could steel
To spray these innocents out of a meal?
My heart is mush, so come on, larvæ,
My closet's full, and I'm Fred Harvey.

Once there was a man named Mr. Weaver,
And he had a lot of hay but he didn't have any hay fever,
So he ran an advertisement which he wanted to charge, but
    for which he was compelled to pay,
And he advertised that he would like to meet up with
    somebody who had a lot of hay fever but didn't have
    any hay,
So along came a man and he said he had seen his ad in the
    paper,
And was the proposition serious or merely a prankish caper,
And Mr. Weaver said it was as serious as the dickens,
Because to his mind hay fever was to the human race what
    bumblefoot, limber neck and edema of the wattles
    were to chickens,
And he said he was the most modest of men,
But never having had hay fever he felt very irked at being
    outexperienced by any passing bumblefooted hen,
And the man said I can describe hay fever for you so you'll
    know all about it but first how much are you prepared
    to pay?
And Mr. Weaver said, "Can I charge it?" and the man said
    No, so Mr. Weaver said he would give him all his
    hay,
So the man said All right and threw pepper in Mr.
    Weaver's eyes,
And Mr. Weaver said, "What are you doing?" and the
    man said "Never mind, just kindly answer the follow-
    ing questions with the correct replies,
What's the kind of nut you put back in the dish at cock-

tail parties," and Mr. Weaver said "A cashew," and the man said "Gesundheit. What material do politicians say their opponents' lies are composed of?" and Mr. Weaver said "The whole cloth," and the man said "No no try again," and Mr. Weaver said "A tissue," and the man said "Gesundheit. What's a filmy collar often worn by women?" and Mr. Weaver said "A fichu," and the man said "Gesundheit. Now you know all about hay fever,"

So he went off with Mr. Weaver's hay, but first he telephoned an old schoolmate in Vancouver and charged the call to Mr. Weaver.

The further through life I drift

The more obvious it becomes that I am lacking in thrift.

Now thrift is such a boon to its possessor that years ago they began to tax it,

But it is a bane to him that lacks it

Because if you lack it you will go into a shoppe and pay two dollars for a gifte,

But if you possess it you find something just as good for a dollar fifte.

A penny is merely something that you pull several of out of your pocket before you find the nickel you need for a telephone call, if thriftlessness is in your blood,

Whereas to the thrifty a penny is something to be put out at stud.

Thrifty people put two-cent stamps on letters addressed to a three-cent zone,

And thriftless people on the other end pay the postage due and the thrifty people chuckle and rub their hands because the saving on every six letters represents a year's interest on a dollar loan.

Oh that I were thrifty, because thrifty people leave estates to delight their next of kin with;

Oh yes that I were thrifty, because then not only would I have money in the bank to pay my bills, but I could leave the money in the bank because I wouldn't have run up the bills to begin with;

Oh that I were not a spendthrift, oh then would my heart
 indeed be gladsome,
Because it is so futile being a spendthrift because I don't
 know any places where thrift could be spent even if I
 had some.

BOO!

The male mosquito fills the air
With threats of eating babies rare;
His humming, like a jackal's bark,
Harrows children in the dark;
But listen, kids, it's all all right,
The male mosquito cannot bite.
Thus we compare the male mosquito
To people who — Why, here's Benito!

All good men believe that women would rather get rid of a
    piece of gossip than a bulge,

And all good women believe that gossip is a feminine
    weakness in which men never indulge.

Rather than give ear to scandalous rumors,

Why, men would rather play golf in bloomers,

And rather than talk behind each other's backs,

They would go shopping in a mink coat and slacks.

It is one of each sex's uniquenesses

That men's talk is all of humanity's aspirations, and
    women's all of their friends' weaknesses.

Yes, this is a universal credo that no amount of evidence
    can alter,

Including that of Petronius, Suetonius, Pepys, Boswell, the
    locker room of the country club, and Mrs. Winchell's
    little boy, Walter.

Allow me to ask and answer one question before depart-
    ing for Mount Everest or Lake Ossipee:

Who says men aren't gossipy? — Men say men aren't
    gossipy.

I do not know its name.
Mostly it's called The Game.

Or sometimes Indications,
Or other variations.

But whatever be its name,
I was happy ere it came.

But now that it has come,
I'm a bum.

Figure of fun and shame,
I do not like The Game.

To be honest, to be candid,
I do not understandid;

I amn't very good at it,
I'm never understood at it.

I am seized by mental gout
When acting phrases out.

I am lost in foggy mazes
When guessing others' phrases.

I'm a gabbling babbling moron
At quotations from The Koran.

Yea, even Mother Goose's
Leave me stammering excuses.

Be mine, be mine the blame,
But I do not like the game.

Before the game arrived
My social talent thrived.

At chitchat, bridge or poker,
An admitted okeydoker.

A fourteenth at every party
Whether Babbitty or arty.

Where is that talent now,
Inquires this erstwhile wow?

Where is it now? inquiahs
This lowest of pariahs.

And hostesses exclaim
It has vanished with The Game,
The Game without a name,
The Game, The Game, The Game,
You were Beebe ere it came,
But now that it has come
You're a bum.

I do not know its name;
Mostly it's called The Game.

Many enjoy it vastly,
I find it ghastly.

Sleep is something about which I feel so strongly and affectionately that I would fain write a song about it,

And I constantly marvel at the great men who have been wrong about it.

Critics tell us that there have been few more lucid minds than Dr. Johnson's,

Yet it was Dr. Johnson who said, "Preserve me from unseasonable and immoderate sleep," which is obviously arrant nonsense.

What does he mean "unseasonable," does he mean he only wants to sleep in the winter, like a groundhog, or through a Beethoven sonata, like a jitterbug, and does he deem thirteen hours' sleep a night immoderate?

Why Shakespeare himself, whose mind critics tell us there have been few more lucid than, expressly states that "Sleep knits up the ravelled sleave of care" and would be the first to admit that a good thirteen-hour sleep would not only knit it up but even spell it correctly and solder it.

Yet even Shakespeare nodded at times, for did he not write "To sleep: perchance to dream: ay, there's the rub"? Well, he must have written those lines either to Sweeney or the marines or the Thibetan navy,

Because to dream is not the rub, it's the gravy,

Because I know a man, he can't throw a baseball any harder than your granddaughter can blow a bubble,

And he dreamed he was pitching for the Giants against Brooklyn and he shut them out with one hit and it would have been a no-hitter only Mel Ott misjudged

an easy fly with two out in the ninth and it rolled
through his legs for a double,
But he fanned Medwick on two pitched balls to end the
game, so this dream not only pleased him but also
helped the Giants' box office quite a lot,
Because now whenever this man is awake he goes up to
the Polo Grounds not because he expects to get to
pitch again, but just to boo Ott.
So about the greatness of Shakespeare and Dr. Johnson
I do not wish to hear another peep,
Because for my money no man is greater than his respect
for sleep.

THE JELLYFISH

Who wants my jellyfish?
I'm not sellyfish!

Once there was a couple named Mr. and Mrs. Pepperloaf
    and they were simply devoted,
Because each other was upon what they doted,
And in Mrs. Pepperloaf's eyes Mr. Pepperloaf could never
    err,
And he admitted only one flaw in her,
But it was a flaw which took many virtues to assuage,
Consisting in always asking him the date while she was
    reading the paper with the date clearly printed on
    every page,
And whenever he called her attention to this least ad-
    mirable of her traits
She would retort that he didn't trust the paper's weather
    forecasts so then why should she trust its dates.
For eleven years his patience held
But finally he rebelled.
It was on the evening of Friday the seventh that she looked
    up from her paper and asked him the date,
And he replied firmly that she would find it at the top of
    the page so she looked at the top of the page and that
    was that, and presently they sat down to supper and
    ate,
And they were miserable because they had never disagreed
    and this contretemps was a beginner for them,
And at nine his employer's wife called up to ask where
    were they, she and eleven guests were waiting dinner
    for them,
And Mr. Pepperloaf asked Mrs. Pepperloaf how she could
    have so misreckoned,

And she said she knew that they had been invited out on
      the seventh but, according to the newspaper he had
      instructed her to consult, tonight was only the second,
And he picked up the paper and it was last week's, not to-
      day's,
And she said certainly, she had just been reading over some
      recipes for different delicious soufflés,
And now she found the first flaw in him because she had
      obeyed his order to look for the date in the paper,
      hadn't she, so his irritation was uncalled for and un-
      seasonable.
Women would rather be right than reasonable.

THE CARAWAY SEED

The Abbé Voltaire, alias Arouet,
Never denounced the seed of the caraway;
Sufficient proof, if proof we need,
That he never bit into a caraway seed.

Is it true what they say about Los Angeles, that Los Angeles is erratic,

That in the sweet national symphony of common sense
Los Angeles is the static?

Yes it is true, Los Angeles is not only erratic, not only
erotic,

Los Angeles is crotchety, centrifugal, vertiginous, esoteric
and exotic.

Many people blame the movies and the movie makers for
Los Angeles's emotional rumpus,

But they are mistaken, it is the compass.

Certainly Los Angeles is a cloudburst of nonsequiturs, and
of logic a drouth,

But what can you expect of a city that is laid out east and
west instead of north and south?

Mother Nature knows best,

And it was Mother Nature who decreed that all sensible
things run north and south, not east and west.

North is uphill and south is downhill, which is why where
a river springs forth,

That's north,

And where's its mouth,

That's south,

Which is why the Los Angeles mind does not function in
the normal true and tried ways,

Because their city runs east and west instead of north
and south so they approach every decision sideways.

The only solution is for Los Angeles to pivot,

And I imagine the Chamber of Commerce will replace the
divot.

CELERY

Celery, raw,
Develops the jaw,
But celery, stewed,
Is more quietly chewed.

Some people are born simply to pay postage due,

Which is like being born simply to tread on the gum that
other people chew.

Anybody sensible

Knows that the demand for extra postage heralds the arrival of tidings unconditionally dispensable;

There is no instance thus far

Of a postage-due envelope having contained either a check
or a confession of murder or an invitation to dine
with Winston Churchill and Hedy Lamarr;

Yet who so thrifty

As not to pay their own weight in pennies annually to discover that a new grocery store will open week before
last, or that they owe an old grocery store eleven-fifty?

It is postage-due mail that requests your presence at a
benefit and encloses two tickets that will be charged to
you unless you write a letter returning them to the
requester;

It is postage-due mail that electrifies you with a full report
of the graduation exercises at the kindergarten that
you attended, while going on five, for one semester.

Yet such is the fascination of getting nothing for something that whenever the postman whistles,

People pour forth to proffer good money for misdirected
and understamped epistles.

I know a man whose moral sense is checkered,

And next to looking through keyholes he likes reading
other people's mail, but not their postage-due mail, he
says he'd rather browse in the Congressional Record.

ASSORTED CHOCOLATES

If some confectioner were willing
To let the shape announce the filling,
We'd encounter fewer assorted chocs,
Bitten into and returned to the box.

PRACTICALLY A SUMMARY OF
PRACTICALLY AUTUMN

September is a curious month,
It has no sense at all, yet.
It's not precisely summer,
But it's not exactly fall, yet.

A curious month September is.
Its weather is its highlight;
You roll your shirtsleeves up at noon
And don your furs at twilight.

September is a curious month.
It made the nations brothers
By awarding one the Davis Cup
And enraging all the others.

A curious month September is.
Its sports will not stay put, now;
Among its ball games, half are base —
And half of them are foot — now.

September is a curious month.
With winter drawing sooner,
The ladies buy new thingumajigs
Not Decemberer, but Juner.

A curious month September is.
Regret is what it ends with,
And yet relief is partly what
We part from summer friends with.

September is a curious month,
Which I wouldn't part with a day from.
It makes you glad to get back to where
You were glad to get away from.

It's more than logical, it's biological,
To be lethargical,
And contrariwise it's abecedarian, or childishly alpha-
     betic,
That it's ridiculous to be energetic.
Welcome, lassitude!
Scram, vivacitude!
Up with the grasshopper and the sluggard!
Away with the ant and the bee and all individualists
     whether puny or ruggard!
Before our ancestors were apes they were fish,
But they improved their condition and got to be human
     beings and founded a lot of empires such as the an-
     cient Persian and Roman and the contemporary Brish,
But the ocean today with us would be brimming
If our ancestors hadn't had sense enough to stop all that
     continuous swimming,
Whereas now we can ride up and down in elevators and go
     to the movies, and fish are only something about
     which some people say, "Yum yum, right out of the
     water and fried to a delicate golden brown,"
And the only reason the fish aren't eating the people in-
     stead of the people eating the fish is that fish can't do
     two things that have got people where they are, they
     can't close their eyes and they can't sit down.

THE PARSNIP

The parsnip, children, I repeat,
Is simply an anemic beet.
Some people call the parsnip edible;
Myself, I find this claim incredible.

The song about the happy-go-lucky fellow who hasn't time
to be a millionaire strikes me as pretty funny,

Because I am pretty happy-go-lucky myself but it isn't lack
of time that keeps me from being a millionaire, it's
lack of money,

But if anybody has a million that they're through with it,

Well, I know what I'd like to do with it.

My first acquisition would not be a lot of Old Masters or
first editions or palatial palaces,

No, it would be to supply each of my pairs of pants with its
own set of galluses.

I can also think of another extravagance with which to
startle all beholders

Which is an attendant with no other duties than to apply
antisunburn lotion to that vulnerable spot you can't
get at yourself either by reaching over or under your
shoulders.

Likewise I have an idea which should earn the gratitude of
every regular-dinner eater alive,

Which is to promote a regular-dinner that when you order
oysters or clams on it you get six oysters or clams instead of five.

My next goal is one to reach which I should probably have
to sink into debt,

But it would be worth it because it is the development
of a short, hot, harsh, quick-burning, full-of-nicotine
cigarette.

A million dollars could also be well spent in hiring somebody to invent some better rhymes for wife than rife and knife and strife,

But I think what I would really do if I had a million would be to buy a million dollars' worth of books written by me and then besides having a lot of good books I could sit back and live on the royalties for the rest of my life.

So it comes to pass

That you double up with the neighbors to save rubber and gas,

And who are you to pity that celluloid dog in pursuit of that asbestos cat?

Your automobile-mate turns out to be nice old Mr. Platt,

And nice old Mr. Platt is no Casey Jones, he is even no nice old Judge Hardy,

When he calls for you he is fifteen minutes early, and when you call for him he is fifteen minutes tardy,

And he has worn a depression in the front seat of your car, but in his, no matter how you fumble,

Well, somehow you always end up with your knees against your chin back in his roofed-in rumble,

And if you are driving, why the task of pointing out oncoming vehicles and curves is one he is too conscientious to spurn,

And if he is driving he never remembers where he wants to turn left until he is halfway past the left turn,

And it's an odd thing about nice old Mr. Platt and the crack of dawn,

Because if you find an evening tedious, the crack of dawn is the moment to which he intends to linger on,

While if you are enjoying yourself, at nine o'clock he will smother a yawn,

And explain that he is sorry to drag you away but unfortunately he has an important engagement at the crack of dawn.

Oh well, I guess that's that —

Some people are doubled up with ptomaine, and other people are doubled up with nice old Mr. Platt.

THE PORPOISE

I kind of like the playful porpoise,
A healthy mind in a healthy corpus.
He and his cousin, the playful dolphin,
Why they like swimmin like I like golphin.

THE SHARK

How many Scientists have written
The shark is gentle as a kitten!
Yet this I know about the shark:
His bite is worser than his bark.

WATER FOR THE GANDER

You take a man who has ever possessed an infant son or
daughter,
And he feels pretty superior about drinks of water.
His voice is full of paternal lenience
As he describes how their thirst is always adjusted to his
utmost inconvenience,
And you gather that there is no rest for the married,
If only because of the little ones who choose to be per-
petually inopportunely arid.
I assume that these little ones have never seen their sire in
session
At his business or profession,
So listen closely, infant son and infant daughter,
His business or profession is what he carries on between
getting up to get a drink of water.
It requires a dozen visits to the nearest water cooler or
fount
Before he can face drawing up a report or balancing an ac-
count.
You may be interested to note
That the driest point in America is not Death Valley, but
a man with lots of important work on his desk's throat.
Therefore, children, when he next complains at midnight
about your everlasting thirst,
Simply ask him how many hours he spent that day at his
desk and how many at the water cooler, and he may
answer you, but I bet he has to go and get himself a
drink of water first.

THE CANTALOUPE

One cantaloupe is ripe and lush,
Another's green, another's mush.
I'd buy a lot more cantaloupe
If I possessed a fluoroscope.

How many years to Bethlehem?
Near a hundred score.
Can I get there by candlelight?
Not this war.

The friendly, holy candle light
Is bale fire now to death,
Its perilous glimmer long blown out
By sirens' breath.

Through skies the Wise Men humbly scanned
Three keener hunters flit —
Heinkel and Dornier seek the gleam,
With Messerschmitt.

No manger now, no cattle shed,
Too lowly to be found.
Take up the babe and hurry him
Deep underground.

But cave nor grave is deep enough
To shield young flesh and bone.
Hurry him down, and o'er his head
Roll the great stone.

What need of law to still the bells,
For how should bells be merry?
The day the child in joy was born,
The child we bury.

Gentlemen of the High Command,
Who crucify the slums,
There was an earlier Golgotha.
The third day comes.

I know a man who when he bares his breast to life it comes
    back to him all covered with welts,

Because everything that happens to him is much worse
    than the same thing happening to anybody else.

Other people with a cold just have colds, but when he has
    a cold it combines pneumonia and dropsy and tropi-
    cal fever,

And he greets any attempt to cheer him up with the frigid
    politeness of a retiring Chairman of the Board saying
    How do you do to the newly appointed Receiver.

Other people with indigestion just have indigestion, but
    his indigestion ranks somewhere between appendicitis
    and cholera,

And his medicine chest is clogged with various gastric ap-
    peasers costing from fifty cents a bottle up to a dol-
    lar a.

He is the man for whom the razor-blade people manu-
    facture that special individual teaspoon-edged blade
    for,

And the man who never discovers that his new shoes don't
    fit until immediately after they are paid for.

Everybody is always running around with bushels with
    which to hide his talents,

And he is the only depositor in the world for whom his
    bank employs a special staff of certified private ac-
    countants just to keep his bank book out of balance.

I really don't see how that man remains perpendicular,

And I am glad that I am not at all like him, except in many
    a particular.

THE OCTOPUS

Tell me, O Octopus, I begs,
Is those things arms, or is they legs?
I marvel at thee, Octopus;
If I were thou, I'd call me Us.

There is one point which I am more than human on,
And that's a noumenon.
On due reflection we are apt to find
That it is noumenons which lead us to believe that just
 this once two pair will beat three of a kind.
It is noumenons which whisper to our hearts that our fu-
 tures will be brighter than our yores,
And noumenons which encourage us to laugh off the black
 clouds in the west and go ahead and move the supper
 table out of doors.
It is noumenons which convince you that you can meet
 the next tax installment without having set aside the
 sum that is requisite,
And noumenons which stir the fancy that M. Laval may
 someday reject an order from Berlin with a cry of
 "Ze hequisite."
It is noumenons which, if you have no excuse for flouting
 natural laws, they supply it,
Such as kindling the hope that you can remain trim and lissome at forty without the nuisance of exercise or diet,
So now I shall go out and consume a hearty lunch,
But I know I shall remain trim and lissome in spite of it,
 because I have a strong noumenon, or overwhelming
 hunch.

* Noumenon, n., an object known only by intuition, apart from
any evidence of the senses.

THE MERMAID

Say not the mermaid is a myth,
I knew one once named Mrs. Smith.
She stood while playing cards or knitting;
Mermaids are not equipped for sitting.

A BULLETIN HAS JUST COME IN

The rabbit's dreamy eyes grow dreamier
As he quietly gives you tularemia.

The parrot clashes his hooked proboscis
And laughs while handing you psittacosis.

In every swamp or wooded area
Mosquito witches brew malaria.

We risk at every jolly picnic
Spotted fever from a tick nick.

People perish of bubonic;
To rats, it's better than a tonic.

The hog converted into pork
Puts trichinosis on your fork.

The dog today that guards your babies
Tomorrow turns and gives them rabies.

The baby, once all milk and spittle,
Grows to a Hitler, and boy, can he hittle!

That's our planet, and we're stuck with it.
I wish its inheritors the best of luck with it.

The world contains so many beautiful things to gaze at
That gazing is an occupation that you could spend days at,
And these beautiful things are of so many different kinds,
    or shall we say heterogeneous,
Such as the sun and moon etc. and butterflies and mer-
    maids etc. that to list them all you would have to be
    an et-cetera genius,
So I shall hasten to a landing
And mention two beautiful things that are to my mind
    outstanding,
And one of them is to be on a train,
And see what we see when we flatten our noses against the
    pane,
And the other is wistful enough to make anybody feel cos-
    mic and pious,
Which is to stand beside the track and wave at the passen-
    gers as they rocket by us,
So that is why rather than be an et-cetera or any other kind
    of genius
I would rather be schizophrenious,
Because I should regard it as the most satisfactory of stunts
To be able to split my personality and be in two places at
    once,
For who could be so happy as I
Sitting with my nose against a train window watching me
    wave to me as I go rocketing by?

THE EEL

I don't mind eels
Except as meals.

Once there was a golfer named Mr. Brownie and he was a
    duffer,

And he used to suffer,

But I don't want to be misunderstood,

He suffered chiefly not because he was bad but because he
    thought he was good,

Because his regular game was 101 and if he had never
    broken 100 his disposition would have been fine,

But one day eleven years ago playing winter rules with a
    following wind and a dozen conceded putts he turned
    in an 89.

Since when he has never been the same,

Because he has ever since been off his game.

And once there was a railroad named the Baltimore and
    Tomsk and it too had grandiose delusions,

And it jumped at conclusions,

And although no one to the B. & T. than I could be loy-
    aler,

I am sorry that they once made a four-hour nonstop run
    between Tomsk and Baltimore with a locomotive and
    baggage car, paced by a motor cycle, with the en-
    gineer smoking marihuana, and benzedrine in the
    boiler,

Because now they think they can dispatch a fourteen-car
    train with six scheduled stops and a flag stop and its
    time between Tomsk and Baltimore will still be the
    same,

And they quote four hours as their regular running time
    just as Mr. Brownie quotes 89 as his regular game.

*Does it please you, dear B. & T., that your timetable
should be Mr. Brownie's score-card's mate?
Remember that a passenger would rather arrive on time on
a four hour and fifty minute schedule than expect a
four-hour trip and arrive fifty minutes late.*

THE WASP

The wasp and all his numerous family
I look upon as a major calamity.
He throws open his nest with prodigality,
But I distrust his waspitality.

NOT GEORGE WASHINGTON'S, NOT
ABRAHAM LINCOLN'S, BUT MINE

Well, here I am thirty-eight,

Well, I certainly thought I'd have longer to wait.

You just stop in for a couple of beers,

And gosh, there go thirty-seven years.

Well, it has certainly been fun,

But I certainly thought I'd have got a lot more done.

Why if I had been really waked up and alive,

I could have been a Congressman since I was twenty-one
    or President since I was thirty-five.

I guess I know the reason my accomplishments are so
    measly:

I don't comprehend very easily.

It finally dawned on me that in life's race I was off to a de-
    layed start

When at the age of thirty-three I had to be told that I
    could swim faster if I'd keep my fingers together in-
    stead of spreading them apart,

And I was convinced that precociousness was not the chief
    of my faults

When it was only last winter that I discovered that the
    name of that waltz that skaters waltz to is "The
    Skaters' Waltz."

After thirty-seven years I find myself the kind of man that
    anybody can sell anything to,

And nobody will ever tell anything to.

Whenever people get up a party of which I am to be a
    member to see some picture which I don't want to see

because I am uninterested in the situation that Scar-
lett and Mr. Chips are estranged over,
Why my head is what it is arranged over.
Contrariwise, I myself not only can't sell anybody any-
thing,
I can't even ever tell anybody anything.
I have never yet had a good gossip bomb all poised and
ready to burst
That somebody hasn't already told everybody first.
Yes, my career to date has certainly been a fiasco;
It would not have made a thrilling dramatic production for
the late Oliver Morosco or the late David Belasco.
But in spite of the fact that my career has been a fiasco to
date,
Why I am very proud and happy to be thirty-eight.

THE KANGAROO

O Kangaroo, O Kangaroo,
Be grateful that you're in the zoo,
And not transmuted by a boomerang
To zestful tangy Kangaroo meringue.

If there are any wives present who wish to irritate their hus-
    bands or husbands who wish to irritate their wives,
Why I know an irritation more irritating than hives,
So if you think such an irritation expedient,
Here is the formula, in which the presence of a third per-
    son is the only essential extra ingredient;
Indeed it is beautifully simple,
But it is guaranteed to make a molehill out of a dimple
And what it consists of is that when you are annoyed with
    your husband or wife and want to do the opposite of
    woo them,
Why, you just talk at them instead of to them.
Suppose you think your Gregory danced too often with
    Mrs. Limbworthy at the club, you don't say to him
    directly, "Gregory I'll smack you down if you don't
    lay off that platinum-plated hussy,"
No, you wait till a friend drops in and then with a glance
    at Gregory say to her, "Isn't it funny what fools
    middle-aged men can make of themselves over any-
    thing blonde and slithery, do you understand how
    anybody sober and in their right mind could look
    twice at that Limbworthy job, but then of course dar-
    ling, Gregory wasn't altogether in his right mind last
    night, was he?"
This is indeed more excruciating to Gregory than Shake-
    spearian excursions and alarums,
Because there is no defense against caroms.
Or let us suppose you are irked by your Esmeralda's sudden
    passion for antiques.

Well you don't mention it for weeks,

No, you wait till a friend drops in and then with a glance
at Esmeralda you say, "How anybody can be sucked
in by this antique racket is beyond me, but there are
some otherwise sensible women who'll mortgage their
beauty treatments for a genuine early American paper
doily or a guaranteed second-hand Killarney banshee,

But of course Esmeralda can't ever resist an opportunity
to pick up some fossil to amaze her friends with, can
she?"

And Esmeralda must sit quiet and take it with apparent
docility,

Because the hit direct doesn't compare with the ricochet in
deadly unanswerability.

By this easy method can every Gregory score off every
Esmeralda and every Esmeralda annihilate every
Gregory,

And its only drawback besides eventual divorce is that it
reduces all their friends to emotional beggary.

FURTHER REFLECTION ON PARSLEY

Parsley
Is gharsley.

I'LL WRITE THEIR NUMBER DOWN WHEN
WE GET HOME

Words, idle words, are what people's social life contains
a goodly store of,
And the idlest words are contained in the wishful phrase
beginning, Why don't we see more of?
By the time your age is medium,
Well, your most exotic evenings are placid to the point of
tedium,
Because whenever you step out you find yourself stepping
out amid faces and ideas that are, to say the least,
familiar,
Which is a situation which moves only from the willy-nilly
to the willy-nillier,
But once in every eleven blue moons you encounter a new-
comer in your little coterie,
And it doesn't matter whether he is a veteran or a veteri-
nary or a vestryman or a vegetarian or a notable or a
Notogæan or a notary,
Because his fresh point of view is as beneficial to anemic
conversation as a transfusion or a tonic,
And his wife is equally attractive and stimulating, and the
future would be cute as a button if it weren't so in-
evitably ironic,
Because on the way home you say "My I like those people,
why don't we see more of them?" and it is agreed that
Yes we certainly must, and from then on they might
as well be living in the ancient Anglian kingdom of
Mercia,
Because you never see them again because you never do

anything about it except to murmur "Why don't we see more of them?" and that is why the best definition I can think of for at least one man's social life is simply inertia.

THE FLY

God in His wisdom made the fly
And then forgot to tell us why.

Now that they've abolished chrome work
I'd like to call their attention to home work.
Here it is only three decades since my scholarship was
    famous,
And I'm an ignoramus.
I cannot think which goes sideways and which goes up and
    down, a parallel or a meridian,
Nor do I know the name of him who first translated the
    Bible into Indian, I see him only as an enterprising
    colonial Gideon.
I have difficulty with dates,
To say nothing of the annual rainfall of the Southern Cen-
    tral States,
And the only way I can distinguish proper from improper
    fractions
Is by their actions.
Naturally the correct answers are just back of the tip of my
    tongue,
But try to explain that to your young.
I am overwhelmed by their erudite banter,
I am in no condition to differentiate between Timoshenko
    and Tam o' Shanter.
I reel, I sway, I am utterly exhausted;
Should you ask me when Chicago was founded I could
    only reply I didn't even know it was losted.

THE BOY WHO LAUGHED AT SANTA CLAUS

In Baltimore there lived a boy.
He wasn't anybody's joy.
Although his name was Jabez Dawes,
His character was full of flaws.
In school he never led his classes,
He hid old ladies' reading glasses,
His mouth was open when he chewed,
And elbows to the table glued.

He stole the milk of hungry kittens,
And walked through doors marked No ADMITTANCE.
He said he acted thus because
There wasn't any Santa Claus.
Another trick that tickled Jabez
Was crying "Boo!" at little babies.
He brushed his teeth, they said in town,
Sideways instead of up and down.

Yet people pardoned every sin,
And viewed his antics with a grin,
Till they were told by Jabez Dawes,
"There isn't any Santa Claus!"
Deploring how he did behave,
His parents swiftly sought their grave.
They hurried through the portals pearly,
And Jabez left the funeral early.

Like whooping cough, from child to child,
He sped to spread the rumor wild:

"Sure as my name is Jabez Dawes
There isn't any Santa Claus!"
Slunk like a weasel or a marten
Through nursery and kindergarten,
Whispering low to every tot,
"There isn't any, no there's not!"

The children wept all Christmas Eve
And Jabez chortled up his sleeve.
No infant dared hang up his stocking
For fear of Jabez' ribald mocking.
He sprawled on his untidy bed,
Fresh malice dancing in his head,
When presently with scalp a-tingling,
Jabez heard a distant jingling;
He heard the crunch of sleigh and hoof
Crisply alighting on the roof.

What good to rise and bar the door?
A shower of soot was on the floor.
What was beheld by Jabez Dawes?
The fireplace full of Santa Claus!
Then Jabez fell upon his knees
With cries of "Don't," and "Pretty please."
He howled, "I don't know where you read it,
But anyhow, I never said it!"

"Jabez," replied the angry saint,
"It isn't I, it's you that ain't.
Although there is a Santa Claus,
There isn't any Jabez Dawes!"

Said Jabez then with impudent vim,
"Oh, yes there is; and I am him!
Your magic don't scare me, it doesn't" —
And suddenly he found he wasn't!

From grimy feet to unkempt locks
Jabez became a jack-in-the-box,
An ugly, vastly ghastly jack
In Santa Claus's bulging pack.
The neighbors heard his mournful squeal;
They searched for him, but not with zeal.
No trace was found of Jabez Dawes,
Which led to thunderous applause,
And people drank a loving cup
And went and hung their stockings up.

All you who sneer at Santa Claus,
Beware the fate of Jabez Dawes,
The saucy boy who mocked the saint.
Donder and Blitzen licked off his paint.

THE TERMITE

Some primal termite knocked on wood
And tasted it, and found it good,
And that is why your Cousin May
Fell through the parlor floor today.

Nothing is glummer
Than a cold in the summer.
A summer cold
Is to have and to hold.
A cough in the fall
Is nothing at all,
A winter snuffle
Is lost in the shuffle,
And April sneezes
Put leaves on the treeses,
But a summer cold
Is to have and to hold.
Though golf course and beach
Slip beyond your reach,
By a fate grotesque
You can get to your desk,
And there is no rescue
From this germ grotesque.
You can feel it coming
In your nasal plumbing,
But there is no plumber
For a cold in the summer.
Nostrilly, tonsilly,
It prowls irresponsilly;
In your personal firmament
Its abode is permament.
Oh, would it were curable
Rather than durable;
Were it Goering's or Himmler's,

Or somebody simlar's!
O Laval, were it thine!
But it isn't, it's mine.
A summer cold
Is to have and to hold.